THEOL

CW00693294

The range of Theodor Adorno's achievement and the depth of his insights are breathtaking and daunting. His work on literary, artistic and musical forms, his devastating indictment of modern industrial society, and his profound grasp of Western culture from Homer to Hollywood have made him one of the most significant figures in twentieth-century thought.

As one of the main philosophers of the Frankfurt School of Critical Theory, Adorno's influence on literary theory, cultural studies and philosophical aesthetics has been immense. His wide-ranging authorship is significant also to continental philosophy, political theory, art criticism and musicology. Key ideas discussed in this guide include:

- art and aesthetics
- fun and free time
- nature and reason
- things, thought and being right

This *Routledge Critical Thinkers* guide will equip readers with the tools required to interpret critically Adorno's major works, while also introducing them to his interpretation of classical German philosophy and his relationship to the most significant of his contemporaries.

Ross Wilson is Leverhulme Trust Early Career Fellow in the Faculty of English, Cambridge University, and Fellow of Emmanuel College. His research interests include the history and theory of literary criticism, philosophical aesthetics, British Romantic poetry and poetics, and eighteenth-century and Romantic theories of language.

ROUTLEDGE CRITICAL THINKERS

Series Editor: Robert Eaglestone, Royal Holloway,
University of London

Routledge Critical Thinkers is a series of accessible introductions to key figures in contemporary critical thought.

With a unique focus on historical and intellectual contexts, the volumes in this series examine important theorists':

- significance
- motivation
- key ideas and their sources
- impact on other thinkers

Concluding with extensively annotated guides to further reading, *Routledge Critical Thinkers* are the student's passport to today's most exciting critical thought.

For further details on this series, see www.routledge.com/literature/series.asp

THEODOR ADORNO

Ross Wilson

Routledge
Taylor & Francis Group

LONDON AND NEW YORK

First published 2007
by Routledge
2 Park Square, Milton Park, Abingdon, Oxon OX14 4RN

Simultaneously published in the USA and Canada
by Routledge
711 Third Avenue, New York, NY 10017

Routledge is an imprint of the Taylor & Francis Group, an informa business

Typeset in Perpetua by
Keystroke, 28 High Street, Tettenhall, Wolverhampton

British Library Cataloguing in Publication Data
A catalogue record for this book is available from the British Library

Library of Congress Cataloging in Publication Data
Wilson, Ross.
Theodor Adorno / Ross Wilson.
p. cm. – (Routledge critical thinkers)
Includes bibliographical references (p.) and index.
1. Adorno, Theodor W., 1903–1969. I. Title.
B3199.A34W55 2007
193–dc22
2007027732

ISBN 10: 0–415–41818–6 (hbk)
ISBN 10: 0–415–41819–4 (pbk)
ISBN 10: 0–203–93332–X (ebk)

ISBN 13: 978–0–415–41818–8 (hbk)
ISBN 13: 978–0–415–41819–5 (pbk)
ISBN 13: 978–0–203–93332–9 (ebk)

CONTENTS

CONTENTS

SERIES EDITOR'S PREFACE

The books in this series offer introductions to major critical thinkers who have influenced literary studies and the humanities. The *Routledge Critical Thinkers* series provides the books you can turn to first when a new name or concept appears in your studies.

Each book will equip you to approach a key thinker's original texts by explaining her or his key ideas, putting them into context and, perhaps most importantly, showing you why this thinker is considered to be significant. The emphasis is on concise, clearly written guides which do not presuppose a specialist knowledge. Although the focus is on particular figures, the series stresses that no critical thinker ever existed in a vacuum but, instead, emerged from a broader intellectual, cultural and social history. Finally, these books will act as a bridge between you and the thinker's original texts: not replacing them but rather complementing what she or he wrote.

These books are necessary for a number of reasons. In his 1997 autobiography, *Not Entitled*, the literary critic Frank Kermode wrote of a time in the 1960s:

> On beautiful summer lawns, young people lay together all night, recovering from their daytime exertions and listening to a troupe of Balinese musicians. Under their blankets or their sleeping bags, they would chat drowsily about the gurus of the time ... What they repeated was largely hearsay; hence my lunchtime suggestion, quite impromptu, for a series of short, very

cheap books offering authoritative but intelligible introductions to such figures.

There is still a need for 'authoritative and intelligible introductions'. But this series reflects a different world from the 1960s. New thinkers have emerged and the reputations of others have risen and fallen, as new research has developed. New methodologies and challenging ideas have spread through the arts and humanities. The study of literature is no longer – if it ever was – simply the study and evaluation of poems, novels and plays. It is also the study of the ideas, issues, and difficulties which arise in any literary text and in its interpretation. Other arts and humanities subjects have changed in analogous ways.

With these changes, new problems have emerged. The ideas and issues behind these radical changes in the humanities are often presented without reference to wider contexts or as theories which you can simply 'add on' to the texts you read. Certainly, there's nothing wrong with picking out selected ideas or using what comes to hand – indeed, some thinkers have argued that this is, in fact, all we can do. However, it is sometimes forgotten that each new idea comes from the pattern and development of somebody's thought and it is important to study the range and context of their ideas. Against theories 'floating in space', the *Routledge Critical Thinkers* series places key thinkers and their ideas firmly back in their contexts.

More than this, these books reflect the need to go back to the thinker's own texts and ideas. Every interpretation of an idea, even the most seemingly innocent one, offers its own 'spin', implicitly or explicitly. To read only books on a thinker, rather than texts by that thinker, is to deny yourself a chance of making up your own mind. Sometimes what makes a significant figure's work hard to approach is not so much its style or content as the feeling of not knowing where to start. The purpose of these books is to give you a 'way in' by offering an accessible overview of these thinkers' ideas and works and by guiding your further reading, starting with each thinker's own texts. To use a metaphor from the philosopher Ludwig Wittgenstein (1889–1951), these books are ladders, to be thrown away after you have climbed to the next level. Not only, then, do they equip you to approach new ideas, but they empower you, by leading you back to a theorist's own texts and encouraging you to develop your own informed opinions.

Finally, these books are necessary because, just as intellectual needs have changed, the education systems around the world – the contexts in which introductory books are usually read – have changed radically, too. What was suitable for the minority higher education system of the 1960s is not suitable for the larger, wider, more diverse, high-technology education systems of the twenty-first century. These changes call not just for new, up-to-date introductions but new methods of presentation. The presentational aspects of *Routledge Critical Thinkers* have been developed with today's students in mind.

Each book in the series has a similar structure. They begin with a section offering an overview of the life and ideas of each thinker and explain why she or he is important. The central section of each book discusses the thinker's key ideas, their context, evolution and reception. Each book concludes with a survey of the thinker's impact, outlining how their ideas have been taken up and developed by others. In addition, there is a detailed final section suggesting and describing books for further reading. This is not a 'tacked-on' section but an integral part of each volume. In the first part of this section you will find brief descriptions of the thinker's key works, then, following this, information on the most useful critical works and, in some cases, on relevant websites. This section will guide you in your reading, enabling you to follow your interests and develop your own projects. Throughout each book, references are given in what is known as the Harvard system (the author and the date of a work cited are given in the text and you can look up the full details in the bibliography at the back). This offers a lot of information in very little space. The books also explain technical terms and use boxes to describe events or ideas in more detail, away from the main emphasis of the discussion. Boxes are also used at times to highlight definitions of terms frequently used or coined by a thinker. In this way, the boxes serve as a kind of glossary, easily identified when flicking through the book.

The thinkers in the series are 'critical' for three reasons. First, they are examined in the light of subjects which involve criticism: principally literary studies or English and cultural studies, but also other disciplines which rely on the criticism of books, ideas, theories and unquestioned assumptions. Second, they are critical because studying their work will provide you with a 'tool kit' for your own informed critical reading and thought, which will make you critical. Third, these thinkers are critical because they are crucially important: they deal with ideas and questions which can overturn conventional understandings of the world, of texts, of everything we take for granted, leaving us with a deeper understanding of what we already knew and with new ideas.

No introduction can tell you everything. However, by offering a way into critical thinking, this series hopes to begin to engage you in an activity which is productive, constructive and potentially life-changing.

ACKNOWLEDGEMENTS

I would like to thank Mark Berry, John Hughes, Drew Milne, Josh Robinson, the participants in the Critical Aesthetics conference at Cornell University in April 2006 (especially Robin J. Sowards and Samir Gandesha), and my father, Mike Wilson. David Garrard's comments were, as ever, of the highest value. Robert Eaglestone has been a helpful, encouraging and patient editor, as has Aileen Storry at Routledge. I also thank the Master and Fellows of Emmanuel College, Cambridge, for supporting my work.

I would not have begun writing this book without Simon Jarvis. I am extremely happy to acknowledge my gratitude to him. I would not have finished writing it without the tireless support of my wife, Lesley Wylie. This book is dedicated to her. I alone am to blame for the flaws in it.

ACKNOWLEDGEMENTS

ABBREVIATIONS

AP	'The Actuality of Philosophy'
AT	*Aesthetic Theory*
CI	*The Culture Industry*
CM	*Critical Models*
DE	*Dialectic of Enlightenment*
HTS	*Hegel: Three Studies*
KCA	*Kierkegaard: Construction of the Aesthetic*
KCPR	*Kant's Critique of Pure Reason*
ME	*Against Epistemology: A Metacritique*
MM	*Minima Moralia: Reflections from Damaged Life*
ND	*Negative Dialectics*
NL I	*Notes to Literature*, vol. I
NL II	*Notes to Literature*, vol. II
P	*Prisms*
PDGS	*The Positivist Dispute in German Sociology*
PMP	*Problems of Moral Philosophy*
PNM	*Philosophy of New Music*
SDE	*The Stars Down to Earth*
TLP	'Theses on the Language of the Philosopher'

WHY ADORNO?

Before I can attempt to answer the question 'Why Adorno?' an even more basic and pressing question needs to be addressed: *what* was Theodor W. Adorno (1903–69)? This question has an unusually long list of answers. Adorno was a philosopher, a sociologist, a musicologist, a critic of music and literature, and, indeed, a composer. He was also defined by Hitler's National Socialist regime as being 'of half-Jewish origin' and, in order to avoid otherwise inevitable persecution, became a refugee, first in Great Britain and then in America. Adorno was a prominent intellectual in post-war West Germany, where he was involved in widely broadcast and controversial debates with other intellectual figures. He was a stringent critic of modern society, diagnosing the precariousness of a world with the potential either to establish peace and security for all its inhabitants, or to slide at any moment into unimaginable horror. He died during the period of self-proclaimed revolutionary agitation by the student movements of the late 1960s, with which he had, in many ways, a particularly uncomfortable relationship.

I give neither this list of Adorno's interests nor this indication of the historical circumstances through which he lived in order to daunt you into awe of the subject of this book, although the breadth of those interests and the turmoil of those circumstances are indeed daunting. Rather, it is necessary from the outset to have some understanding of the range of Adorno's interests and concerns, and of the historical context in which they emerged. It is not just the case that we should engage with Adorno's work because he was a remarkably cultured and highly educated German Jew who lived through tumultuous times, although these are already good reasons for reading him. One especially significant reason why Adorno's work is distinctive is that the connections between the apparently quite different areas of his thought are extremely important to the shape and meaning of his work as a whole. It is not simply that Adorno turned his hand to a lot of different intellectual disciplines, but rather that he was especially attentive to the ways in which, for example, literature might be philosophical, in which philosophy might be literary, in which the study of society demands both historical and philosophical reflection. That is, Adorno's literary criticism cannot be separated from his philosophical concerns, which cannot be separated from his theory of society, which, of course, cannot be separated from what he made of the circumstances in which he lived.

Adorno conceives of these connections in an especially radical way but without, crucially, diminishing the importance of the specific features of each area of thought. A work of literature would not, according to Adorno, be of philosophical interest merely because it contains statements, for example, about the existence of the soul, the problem of evil, or the nature of space and time. Were that to be the case, literature would just have been translated, so to speak, into philosophy, and its specific status as literature would have been ignored. For Adorno, the philosophical significance of a work like *Finnegans Wake* by the novelist James Joyce (1882–1941), for example, has much more to do with its narrative form, its diction and syntax, and what it does to the very idea of a work of art, rather than with any pre-established philosophical position that it might be taken to illustrate. This means, for Adorno, that a philosophical interpretation of literature would have to be the closest possible reading of any given text, rather than the identification of whatever general ideas it might be held to contain. A student of literature, then, might read Adorno not for any extractable 'literary theory' but rather for an approach to literature according to which literary criticism already requires the posing and answering of fundamental philosophical questions.

In a similar way, Adorno insists that any theory of society must attend to the details of actual social experience. The best way of elaborating a theory of society is not, in Adorno's view, to turn to general accounts of social trends, but to attend as carefully as possible to what might initially seem to be the insignificant bits and pieces of day-to-day experience. We can learn as much about society when we reflect attentively enough on whether people are in the habit of closing doors behind them when they enter a room or on what people talk about on the train as we can from a pie-chart.

None of this is meant to provide an excuse for breezily ignoring the rigours of academic research and for simply going with your hunch. On the one hand, a significant part of Adorno's work does draw on large-scale sociological research. On the other, intellectual hunches and prejudices, as well as the whole stock of what is established as 'common sense' precisely in order that it not be questioned, is to be as carefully – if not more carefully – scrutinized as anything else.

Saying this does not simply get rid of the dangers that work like Adorno's faces. Thinking like his that insists upon attention to the apparent trivia and detritus of the world, and to the nuances of subjective experience, is liable to be rejected as, precisely, trivial and merely subjective. But before we rush to condemn Adorno as a quirky, self-indulgent essayist, we should ask whether we are really sure that the criteria according to which we would make such a judgement are as reliably objective as we assume.

Adorno aims to combine scrupulous attention to detail with serious reflection on the most apparently abstract philosophical concepts. Indeed, one of the main aims of his thought is to explore – and, ultimately, to question – this division between particular detail and abstract category. This questioning is central to Adorno's understanding of 'dialectic'. (Explanation of this word is one of the main purposes of this book.) The articulation of Adorno's striking commitment to the philosophical significance of those experiences usually dismissed as least worthy of critical thought, along with his tracing of even the most apparently abstract ideas back to actual experience, is one of the main reasons for reading his work.

ADORNO'S INTELLECTUAL DEVELOPMENT

Adorno's distinctive and challenging intellectual vision, which he developed and modified throughout his career, began to be formed remarkably early in his life. He benefited greatly from the cultural and intellectual milieu of early twentieth-century Frankfurt-am-Main, a prosperous, vibrant and liberal city in south-west Germany. Adorno was the precociously talented only child of devoted parents. His father was an assimilated Jew and successful wine-merchant; his Catholic mother had been a celebrated singer from a musically gifted family. Indeed, Adorno's experience of music is one of the most prominent features of his intellectual development. In his youth and early career, Adorno produced a considerable amount of music journalism, including, in particular, reviews of performances of contemporary music. What is striking about this early journalism is its anticipation of some of the central features of Adorno's mature work. Crucially, he refuses to treat music – and art in general – as a pleasant diversion; rather, he wants to consider as strictly as possible the way in which art is related to social conditions, to hope for a better world, and to the idea of truth.

Some readers view the centrality of art and artworks to Adorno's work as something of an embarrassment. Adorno makes very large claims for the significance of art: that it must be seriously considered in terms of truth and untruth; that it has a significant – and complex – relationship to society; and, perhaps most challengingly of all, that it in some sense prefigures a world radically different to this one. This significance of art is not to be located, according to Adorno, in particular statements that artworks make or in positions that they might be seen to represent, but in their specifically artistic characteristics. The influence of Adorno's interest in music in particular is worth mentioning again here. Music does not – unless in the most abstract way – represent or tell us anything, and it does not – at least straightforwardly – contain ideas. (It was for this reason that music was accorded a low rank in certain strands of eighteenth-century aesthetics.) But despite – or, indeed, because of – music's problematic relationship with philosophy, Adorno insists on its intellectual significance. If music can be thought of in terms of its truth or untruth, then the philosophical interpretation of art is not to be directed to the statements that artworks contain, but rather to the way in which artworks are put together, how they are composed. This kind of musically inspired thinking, so to speak, is one of the most difficult and distinctive aspects of Adorno's thought.

The importance of Adorno's early attempts to consider music not just as entertainment but as in some way socially and philosophically meaningful can hardly be overestimated. One of the most important features of his reflection on art generally is that art is not a matter of mere personal taste. His commitment to the philosophical significance of art is complemented by Adorno's sense that philosophy cannot without damage be separated from the way in which it is expressed, that is, from the way in which it is put into words. Indeed, the importance of music in particular to Adorno's characteristic mode of thought again needs to be emphasized. For Adorno, works of philosophy are 'philosophical compositions', and he argues that, as in music, what is important in philosophy is what happens in it – how it develops and unfolds, how certain concerns are reprised – rather than the position-statements that can be extracted from it.

In an essay on his friend, the German sociologist, film critic and novelist Siegfried Kracauer (1889–1966), Adorno recollects how he and Kracauer would meet on Saturday afternoons to read the *Critique of Pure Reason* (first edition, 1781; revised second edition, 1787), by the German philosopher Immanuel Kant (1724–1804) (NL II: 58). There is already something significant in the bare outline of this recollection: Saturday afternoon did not represent, for the young Adorno, a time for idle relaxation but rather for engagement with one of the most important texts in the Western philosophical tradition. As I will show in Chapter 2, Adorno was acutely suspicious of the way that pleasure has become segregated from thinking in modern society, each strictly allotted their own part of the schedule. Indeed, this is one of the most potent claims of Adorno's theory of modern society and culture: that the separation of work from pleasure is fatal to both. Moreover, Adorno and Kracauer read Kant's founding text of modern philosophy in a highly imaginative and unorthodox fashion. For Kracauer, Adorno relates, the point of reading a text like the *Critique of Pure Reason* was not simply to grasp its systematic coherence; rather, the conflicts and contradictions of such a text reveal something about its fundamental motivations and aims. Lecturing on Kant's philosophy in the early 1950s, many years after his initial reading with Kracauer, Adorno noted the difference between his approach to Kant and that of influential commentators such as Klaus Reich (1906–1996) (KCPR: 80). Reich (1992) attempted to establish the systematic coherence and stability of Kant's account of the fundamental structures of human understanding. Adorno states, in contrast to Reich, that he is much more interested in the way that the apparent contradictions in Kant's thinking – which, in more standard philosophical commentary, are ignored, condemned or remedially reinterpreted – reveal something essential about his thought.

What Kracauer had shown Adorno about philosophy was something very different, therefore, from the method in which philosophy was studied in an official, academic setting. Kracauer demonstrated to him that 'the expressive moment in philosophy: putting into words the thoughts that come into one's head' is not a mere inconvenience for the philosopher but rather a crucial aspect of what philosophy is. Adorno recounts that as he came to study philosophy academically he realized that 'among the tensions that are the lifeblood of philosophy the tension between expressiveness and rigor is perhaps the most central' (NL II: 59). What Adorno is claiming is that we must have the utmost attention to the logic of what is said, to the way that it is said, and to the relation between the two. This entails that Adorno is not intimidated by official philosophy's rejection – as mere poetry – of everything that does not meet its established criteria. One of Adorno's chief aims is to examine as closely as possible – without simply overcoming them by an act of will – the divisions whereby philosophy has been separated from its expressive element and, moreover, the divisions according to which intellectual disciplines themselves – philosophy, sociology, literary criticism, history – are each quarantined in their own departments.

ADORNO AND THE INSTITUTE FOR SOCIAL RESEARCH

Adorno's concern with the relations between supposedly discrete intellectual disciplines had a specific institutional setting from early on in his career. Before his exile from Germany, he secured a position with the recently founded Institute for Social Research at Frankfurt University (hence the employees and associates of the institute came to be known as members of the 'Frankfurt School'). Adorno's connection with the institute lasted his entire life and it was to join other exiled members that he went to live in America during the Second World War. According to the statute enshrining the institute's affiliation with the university, its main aims were to foster a particularly comprehensive kind of research into social conditions, including those which prevailed in both the past and the present, and in different countries (see Müller-Doohm: 2005: 516 n.3). From 1931, the head of the institute had been the philosopher and sociologist Max Horkheimer (1895–1973). Adorno's intellectual relationship – and personal friendship – with Horkheimer was to remain fundamental to the development of his work throughout his life. One of the chief concerns central to both Horkheimer and Adorno during the 1930s was precisely what direction the institute should take. Adorno was certainly sympathetic to the aim that individual disciplines – social and political science in particular, but also history and literary criticism – should gain some sort of philosophical impetus as a result of the institute's work. For instance, social science should not simply gather evidence, say, about population densities in certain geographical areas, or about fluctuations in levels of employment in certain industries. It must also interpret these findings from the broader and more essential perspective offered by philosophy (Horkheimer 1993: 1–14). While sympathetic, Adorno had reservations about this kind of aim expressed in this manner, and he thought that it should be qualified in some significant ways. It is not, in Adorno's view, simply philosophy's task to animate specialist disciplines which, although they could do with some help from philosophy to broaden their horizons, are essentially adequate in themselves. Those disciplines are not to receive their philosophical animus, so to speak, from outside. Sociologists, historians and literary critics cannot simply put their feet up once they have collected their data and then wait for a philosopher to come along and do their philosophizing for them. Specialist disciplines devoid of philosophical reflection – and the reasons for how this situation (that is, this division of intellectual labour) has come about – must be submitted to criticism as well as to being helpfully informed by philosophy. It is not good enough for intellectuals to demur from philosophical thinking because it does not fall within their area of competence or because it was not part of their professional training. For Adorno, an intellectual discipline that does its work and then waits for another discipline – philosophy – to come along and animate it cannot be complete in itself. Rather, it is dead.

This quick tour of Adorno's early intellectual development and institutional affiliations is not meant to provide the key to his work. In order fully to master Adorno, one would certainly wish to have some acquaintance with aspects of the work of those writers by whom he was most influenced and with the setting in which he conducted his academic career; I will return to Adorno's relations to a number of prominent philosophers, critics and artists throughout this book. The purpose of this summation of Adorno's intellectual development is to give a sense of the landscape within which his own highly original thought emerged and moved. Adorno quickly – although, of course, with great intellectual effort – developed a distinctive philosophical character and, from the earliest phases of his career, elaborated a number of significant differences from his forebears. Precise demonstration of Adorno's claim on our attention is the burden of the rest of this book.

NOTE ON THE PROCEDURE OF THIS BOOK

Most of the already-published short accounts of Adorno's thinking – and many of the long ones, too – begin with an apology for their existence. This book is no exception. Such an apology is as little false modesty as Adorno's insistence that thinking – especially *his* thinking – cannot be paraphrased is glib self-aggrandisement. What Adorno meant when he argued that thinking cannot be paraphrased is that the way in which philosophy is written is inextricably bound up with its truth and untruth. As we have already seen, this is a lesson that he took from his early reading of Kant with Kracauer. I will explore this insistence on the way in which philosophical truth and philosophical expression are intertwined in greater length at the beginning of Chapter 4.

Given Adorno's suspicions regarding the possibility of paraphrasing his work, a book that attempts to introduce him is faced with a number of difficulties which necessitate potentially irritating – albeit brief – consideration of its own procedure. This book does not offer a general overview of Adorno but rather proceeds by way of attention to some of the specific problems and concerns addressed in his most significant and influential works. This is not to say that it will not address his 'key ideas'; it is to say that those 'key ideas' will be developed through discussion of the detail of those specific questions that Adorno posed and attempted to answer. What this entails, of course, is that this book, like any such introduction, leaves out a lot. However, I attempt to give an indication of some of the ways in which Adorno's work has been received in 'After Adorno' and I give a guide to how areas of his authorship relatively underexamined in this book might be opened up in 'Further Reading'.

KEY IDEAS

KEY IDEAS

1

DISASTER TRIUMPHANT

While I will touch on some of Adorno's early work later, there are good reasons for focusing on *Dialectic of Enlightenment: Philosophical Fragments*, which was first published in 1947, in particular at the beginning. One very simple reason is that this book, which Adorno wrote in exile in California with his colleague Max Horkheimer, remains one of the most innovative and controversial works in the twentieth-century study of culture. In addition, *Dialectic of Enlightenment* includes discussion of concerns that remained central to Adorno throughout his career, as well as a number of striking anticipations of ideas that are only fully explored subsequently.

One question that we might want to ask about this book right at the start is what its main title means. What is 'dialectic' and what is 'enlightenment'? This chapter as a whole explores Adorno and Horkheimer's approach to this question, but we need to have some rough sense of what the terms mean before we get going properly.

First, 'enlightenment'. When it is used to refer to a specific period of intellectual history, 'the Enlightenment' is thought of as that period in which Europe began to emerge from the supposed superstition and irrationality of the Middle Ages, a period which is roughly equivalent with what is usefully called 'the long eighteenth century' (from around the mid-seventeenth century until the last decades of the eighteenth century itself). The Enlightenment in this sense is also often called 'the Age of Reason'. The growth in attempts at systematic scientific explanations of the universe along with an increased insistence on individual and public freedoms are two of the chief characteristics of the Enlightenment. In December 1784, readers of the *Berlinische Monatsschrift* (*Berlin Monthly*) responded to a question which had been posed in a previous issue, which is the question that is concerning us here: 'What is enlightenment?' The response by Immanuel Kant has come to be seen as one of the most important documents of the Enlightenment's self-explanation. '*Enlightenment*', writes Kant, with emphasis, '*is the human being's emergence from his self-incurred immaturity*' (Kant 1996b: 17 [translation modified]). It is important to bear in mind that the German for 'maturity' has both the legal-sounding sense of reaching the age, for example, at which one might come into an inheritance or be granted certain specific rights, and the broader sense of attaining the full development of judgement, thought and action. Conversely, then, what Kant means by 'immaturity' is the inability to use one's reason independently. This inability is not the result of some innate fault but rather of a lack of courage. That is why humankind is to blame for its own unenlightened condition. Kant has a number of suggestions for how enlightenment might be achieved. Fundamental to each of them is an emphasis on the exercise of human reason and freedom.

Thus, the Enlightenment which seemingly flourished during the eighteenth century stressed humanity's essentially rational vocation, its innate freedom, and its ability to know certain things that were previously accounted mysteries. Moreover, the use of reason could tell us not only what to think, but how to act.

While it is certainly of great importance to Adorno and Horkheimer, this understanding of 'enlightenment' does not exhaust what they mean by that term. They argue that any attempt to explain something that has hitherto been held to be rationally inexplicable – that is, any attempt at knowledge that apparently does not have recourse to mystical or otherwise superstitious explanations – is an attempt at enlightenment. Such a view, then, would clearly not confine the idea of 'enlightenment' to the thought and writings of the long eighteenth century. (It is perhaps useful to maintain a distinction – as I have been doing – between 'the Enlightenment', which would name the historical period, and 'enlightenment', understood as a more conceptual designation.) Crucially for Adorno and Horkheimer, enlightenment opposes itself to myth. In particular, enlightenment is aimed at freeing humankind from the fear inherent in mythical ways of construing the world. If I hear something that goes bump in the night, I might think that it is the bogeyman and lose sleep cowering beneath my duvet. If I investigate and discover that a squirrel has got in through a hole in the roof, I will phone Rentokil. My cowering under the duvet is a result of my mythical belief in the bogeyman; my taking rational steps to sort out my rodent problem goes along with my having enlightened myself about the true source of the bump in the night.

This opposition between myth and enlightenment brings us to what Adorno and Horkheimer might mean by a 'dialectic' of enlightenment. Again, like 'enlightenment', 'dialectic' has a significant philosophical pedigree. Perhaps the most important understanding of 'dialectic' upon which Adorno and Horkheimer draw is that developed throughout his work by the German philosopher, G.W.F. Hegel (1770–1831). In his *Logic*, which is the first part of his *Encyclopaedia of the Philosophical Sciences* (first published, 1817; third edition, 1830), for example, Hegel says that 'dialectic' names the way in which apparently simple concepts or propositions ultimately go beyond their own simplicity and turn into their opposites (Hegel 1975b: 115). We can most usefully begin to see what this might mean by considering Adorno and Horkheimer's opposition between enlightenment and myth itself. The argument of their book is that myth is already, in some sense, enlightenment because it is already an attempt at knowledge: the bogeyman is an attempt to explain the bump in the night. Conversely, enlightenment is still myth because, although human beings might have been relieved of their fear of nature, they are increasingly alienated from it and thus an antagonistic relationship with it persists: the squirrel gets it in the neck. Enlightenment can be shown to be characterized by what is allegedly opposed to it; in this way, it is dialectical.

With these rough outlines of what 'dialectic' and 'enlightenment' mean to Adorno and Horkheimer, we can now investigate the central arguments of *Dialectic of Enlightenment* more thoroughly.

THE THESES OF *DIALECTIC OF ENLIGHTENMENT*

The problem that *Dialectic of Enlightenment* addresses seems to be, for such a demanding book, remarkably simple: 'Enlightenment, in the widest sense of progressive thought, has always aimed at liberating men from fear and installing them as masters. Yet the fully enlightened earth is radiant with disaster triumphant' (DE: 1 [translation modified]). This opening definition of 'enlightenment' in some senses echoes the emphatic opening definition of Kant's essay 'What is Enlightenment?' which we looked at a moment ago. Adorno and Horkheimer are far less confident, however, about the straight-forwardness of the course taken by enlightenment. They note that the aim of enlightenment is to liberate humanity from fear. However, although the world is supposedly enlightened, fear still reigns. This is the problem with which *Dialectic of Enlightenment* begins.

It is worth reflecting briefly on this apparently simple pattern of first establishing the problem with which the book is to deal before subsequently tracing it through specific phenomena. To begin with, *Dialectic of Enlightenment* focuses on 'two theses'. That is, it starts with two specific statements which are to be explored more fully in the rest of the book: 'Myth is already enlightenment; and enlightenment reverts to mythology' (DE: xviii). There do not just happen to be two theses in the way that there might have been three, four or twenty. It is perhaps better to think of this as one twofold thesis. The twofold relation of myth to enlightenment is central to the idea that there is a dialectic of enlightenment.

Furthermore, it would be misleading to take too literally Adorno and Horkheimer's statement that 'These theses are worked out in relation to specific subjects in the two excurses' (DE: xviii). (An 'excursus' is a detailed discussion of a particular point arising from a more general account.) What this might seem to suggest is that all the hard intellectual work of the book is done in the opening chapter: that is, the first chapter advances a theoretical position which is then established by way of example in what follows. However, on the one hand, that first chapter, 'The Concept of Enlightenment', is itself concerned with specific phenomena. On the other hand, the following chapters on specific phenomena – which include discussions of episodes from the *Odyssey* by the archaic Greek poet Homer (around eighth century BCE) and of the relation of the novels of the Marquis de Sade (1740–1814) (whose name gives us the word 'sadism', which means the delight in inflicting pain on others) to the principles of enlightened morality – also significantly contribute to and modify the book's argument.

Indeed, Adorno expresses wariness throughout his work of the kind of procedure that would establish its argument first and then come up with examples with which to support it. Perhaps a good way of illuminating this kind of relation between pre-decided conceptual schemes and specific phenomena is through the relation of aesthetics and the philosophy of art to actual artworks. (This relation was one that Adorno considered extensively in his late work *Aesthetic Theory* (posthumously published, 1970), which I will discuss fully in Chapter 3.) Until roughly the middle of the eighteenth century, the philosophy of art was largely concerned to lay down sets of rules for the different arts, including drama, painting, sculpture and architecture. The description by the classical Greek philosopher Aristotle (384–322 BCE) in his *Poetics* of what ought to be included in certain types of poetry, particularly in tragic drama, was almost a compulsory point of reference for any discussion of drama. When actual instances of dramatic writing and performance are held up to the criteria that Aristotle established for supposedly successful drama, all that matters is whether those instances tick the appropriate boxes. Thus, on this view, neo-classical writers like the French playwrights Pierre Corneille (1606–84) and Jean Racine (1639–99) do well because they come closest to following the rules that Aristotle had laid down; Shakespeare, on the other hand, does badly. I do not wish here to question Aristotle's criteria themselves but rather to suggest that such a procedure entails that the rules come first and the specific things that they are supposed to help us understand definitely come second. Adorno is critical of this kind of procedure in which actual particulars are granted much lower rank than the conceptual schemes they are supposed to illustrate. The predominance of abstract systems over particular things has come to mark not just aesthetics, Adorno argues, but the whole of modern reason.

It is important to make this point because, as becomes even clearer in his later work, Adorno criticizes any strict division between general conceptual schemes and the examples which are then slotted into them. The specific phenomena that are dealt with in Adorno's work are there neither to prove an already-established thesis nor (which is basically the same) simply to add colour to an otherwise abstract argument. For Adorno, attention to particular things is much more likely to yield philosophical insight than expending intellectual energy squeezing them into the established patterns they are supposed to fit. Viewing specific phenomena as nothing more than mere illustrations of whatever has already been decided upon is part of the enlightened rationality that Adorno and Horkheimer want to interrogate.

NATURE

Adorno and Horkheimer argue that any account of enlightenment must move beyond the mere affirmation of enlightened ideals. Enlightenment is to be subjected to rigorous scrutiny and, especially, is to be measured by the very standards it professes. The consequences of enlightenment's attempts to overcome fear must be followed through to their ultimate logical conclusions in order to ensure that the concept of enlightenment has been completely grasped. Adorno and Horkheimer claim that merely roping off the assumptions of enlightened rationality as timeless truths and accepting the benevolent image of itself that enlightenment projects fails to do justice to the concept of enlightenment itself. Enlightenment must become enlightened about itself.

Adorno and Horkheimer's critique gets under way by examining how nature is viewed by enlightened reason. Enlightenment reduces the variety of natural phenomena to one basic foundation: nature itself, considered as the mere object of enlightened thought about it and manipulation of it. Thanks to this reduction of natural phenomena to one foundation, reason dominates nature. This reduction of nature to a blank canvas for enlightened reason requires the expulsion of 'immanent powers or hidden properties' from nature (DE: 3). If informed that the woods that are about to be felled in order to make way for another runway are inhabited by 'powers', or that they have unique 'properties' of some sort, modern developers, for example, or the planning officers monitoring their activities, are unlikely to be impressed. Put this way, this may seem like a fairly trivial point but Adorno and Horkheimer argue that enlightenment involves the thoroughgoing expulsion of any inherent meaning from natural phenomena as such. Ultimately, it is by expelling the special properties of individual objects from them that natural phenomena are reduced to one fundamental unit; that is, natural phenomena are reduced to 'matter' or, to put it another way, to 'mere objectivity' (DE: 4, 6).

This reduction of nature to mere matter is part of Adorno and Horkheimer's critique of what has become of the way in which specific phenomena are treated by modern reason. It is not an exaggeration, for Adorno and Horkheimer, to say that there are no longer any specific things for modern reason. This point is illuminated by way of a comparison between, on the one hand, mythical magic, and, on the other, enlightened rational science. Adorno and Horkheimer say that in magic there is 'specific representation' (DE: 6). For example, the sacrificial lamb is meant to stand in for – to deputize for – the first-born child in whose place it is offered up. Likewise, the voodoo doll is meant specifically to represent the enemy of the person sticking the needles into it. These things cannot be swapped for anything else. It is *this* lamb and *this* voodoo doll which stand in for *this* first-born child and *this* enemy. By way of contrast, whatever science manipulates is basically insignificant to it and could just as easily be swapped for another instance of the same kind of thing. The rabbit under the knife of the vivisectionist is not, to the vivisectionist, *this* rabbit but just an example on which to experiment (DE: 7).

It is for this reason that Adorno is wary of 'examples'. He is suspicious of 'examples' if they are merely meant to serve as evidence for a pre-established hypothesis. The rabbit in the laboratory could just as well be replaced by another rabbit, or another relatively docile, predictable animal. Thus, individual natural phenomena have been rendered, in their own right, meaningless. What matters is 'the single relationship between the subject who confers meaning and the meaningless object, between rational significance and its accidental bearer' (DE: 7). Reason alone dictates what is to be declared significant; nothing is significant by itself.

REASON

So far, I have been discussing how Adorno and Horkheimer see reason as having reduced nature to an empty, meaningless vehicle for its own manipulation and domination. But what happens to reason itself in this situation? Reason, the agent of domination, is not immune from the effects of that very domination which it wreaks on nature. Thinking itself takes on particular characteristics as its domination of nature progresses: 'Human beings purchase the increase in their power with estrangement from that over which it is exerted. Enlightenment stands in the same relationship to things as the dictator to human beings. He knows them to the extent that he can manipulate them' (DE: 6). As nature increasingly comes to be dominated the reason that dominates it is more and more separated and distanced – 'estranged' – from what it dominates.

Adorno and Horkheimer elaborate this view in terms of the distinction between subject and object, which we now need to consider more carefully. This aspect of *Dialectic of Enlightenment* is fundamental to the development of Adorno's thinking. Shortly after remarking that one consequence of the domination of nature is *estrangement* of the agent of domination from nature, Adorno and Horkheimer introduce the related idea of 'abstraction': 'the instrument of the enlightenment, [which] stands in the same relationship to its objects as fate, whose concept it eradicates: as liquidation' (DE: 9). This remark is central to understanding Adorno and Horkheimer's argument that enlightenment reverts to mythology. The consequence of enlightened abstraction is, in fact, that objects are treated the same as they were according to the mythical belief in fate. Both fate and abstraction hold absolute sway over the objects to which they relate. Still more importantly for the role of abstraction in enlightenment is abstraction's reliance on one of the central features of enlightened reason: 'the distance of subject from object' (DE: 9). Again, the scientist and the rabbit on the table in front of her or him is a good emblem of this distance. So, too, is the home-owner equipped with the bleach that kills 99 per cent of all known germs and the border-guard armed with the rifle.

The distance between subject and object is the barrier between self and other. According to Adorno and Horkheimer, this distance is anticipated by the distinction between the animate and the inanimate, between living subjectivity and dead nature (DE: 10–11). However, the more that subjectivity posits itself over and against objectivity, the more it becomes like the objectivity which it has drained of any inherent meaning and which it opposes. This objectification of the subject – the way it becomes like the object it attempts to set at a distance – is central to Adorno's account, both in *Dialectic of Enlightenment* and throughout the rest of his work, of modern subjectivity. The chief characteristic of enlightened rationality, therefore, is that it is objectified, that it has become like an object: 'Thought is reified as an autonomous, automatic process, aping the machine it has itself produced, so that it can finally be replaced by the machine' (DE: 19). This sentence does not prophesy some kind of science-fiction nightmare in which machines with artificial intelligence will take over the world. Instead, Adorno and Horkheimer emphasize the way in which thinking makes itself like a machine so that merely mechanical processes of thought come to replace genuine conceptual effort and cognition. Instrumental thinking destroys thinking.

This account of what has become of thinking is connected to Adorno and Horkheimer's view of self-preservation in enlightened rationality. The idea of self-preservation was central, in particular, to Horkheimer's work at around the time of the composition of *Dialectic of Enlightenment* (Horkheimer 1987) and it plays an important role as well throughout Adorno's career, especially in his later works on moral theory, including *Minima Moralia* (1951) and his lectures on *Problems of Moral Philosophy* (lectures delivered, 1963; posthumously published, 1996). Adorno and Horkheimer consider self-preservation in terms of the relation between means (how we achieve something) and end (what we aim to achieve) in enlightened reason. In particular, they focus on how self-preservation turns back on itself to become self-destruction. Adorno and Horkheimer argue that the chief characteristic of the modern self is that it is constituted through a process of renunciation; that is, through a process of giving up things. This is what they mean when they remark that 'The history of civilization is the history of the introversion of sacrifice – in other words, the history of renunciation' (DE: 43). Sacrifice has come to be internalized; I sacrifice (aspects of) myself. The 'identical, enduring self' (DE: 42) relies on the renunciation of the immediate satisfaction of impulse in exchange for its continued existence. The problem with this, according to Adorno and Horkheimer, is that what is given back to the self – its continued existence – is not equivalent to what it has relinquished: 'All who renounce give away more of their life than is given back to them, more than the life they preserve' (DE: 43).

Self-preserving reason that forgets why it preserves itself – or, to put it another way, that gives up everything for which it lives in order merely that it continue to live – becomes self-destructive. This is set out in Adorno and Horkheimer's argument leading up to the statement that the 'history of civilization is the history of the introversion of sacrifice'. This passage is worth quoting in full:

> At the moment when human beings cut themselves off from the consciousness of themselves as nature, all the purposes for which they keep themselves alive – social progress, the heightening of material and intellectual forces, indeed, consciousness itself – become void, and the enthronement of the means as the end, which in late capitalism is taking on the character of overt madness, is already detectable in the earliest history of subjectivity. The human being's mastery of itself, on which the self is founded, practically always involves the annihilation of the subject in whose service that mastery is maintained, because the substance which is mastered, suppressed, and disintegrated by self-preservation is nothing other than the living entity, of which the achievements of self-preservation can only be defined as functions – in other words, self-preservation destroys the very thing which is to be preserved.
>
> (DE: 42–3)

We need to attend to the argument here that self-preservation becomes self-destruction when human reason attempts to cut itself off entirely from human nature; that is, perhaps primarily for Adorno, from the need to avoid pain and the desire for happiness. When human reason is cut off from human nature in this way, self-preservation is established as the end – that is, the aim and purpose – of life itself. Adorno and Horkheimer argue that human reason which has forgotten human nature loses its *raison d'être* precisely because reason was meant to help satisfy the needs of human nature. For Adorno and Horkheimer, it is not at all the case that the satisfaction of material needs and desires is somehow not a concern for reason. Reason that is reason, rather than a merely self-perpetuating mechanism, is meant not simply to enable the continuation of life but rather to make life worth living. Adorno and Horkheimer claim that reason turns back on and destroys itself – and this is the key to this claim – precisely when it seeks to establish itself as purely rational; that is, as entirely divorced from the nature that it has sought to overcome. This view of reason and of its relation to the satisfaction of material needs is central to Adorno's work. Renunciation for the sake of reason of emotional impulses and of the desire for the satisfaction of physical needs not only gives up more than is gained by this renunciation. Such renunciation is itself irrational.

We need now to examine further how reason is implicated in what it would establish – and thus reject – as its opposite.

REASON AND MIMESIS

One of the most important ways in which Adorno and Horkheimer consider reason's continued entanglement with nature is through its relationship to

MIMESIS IN PLATO AND ARISTOTLE

Adorno and Horkheimer do not mean by 'mimesis' what is usually meant by this term. For Plato, especially in his *Republic* and *Ion*, mimesis means 'imitation' in the derogatory sense of superficial similarity to, but ultimate distance from, reality. That is, for Plato, mimesis is imitative in this sense because it is unreal but nevertheless misleadingly like reality. Aristotle, in his *Poetics*, responds to Plato's criticisms of imitation and argues instead that mimesis is 'representation', which, in artistic works, means the representation not of anything actual but of the kinds of things that might be actual. The sense of 'mimesis' still current in philosophy of art is in large part derived from this Platonic and Aristotelian heritage. Contrastingly, Adorno and Horkheimer emphasize much more the idea that 'mimesis' is a kind of 'assimilation' to what is imitated, a becoming like it.

mimesis. As the intellectual historian and chronicler of the Frankfurt School Martin Jay has helpfully emphasized, Adorno's conception of mimesis shuns the idea that a stable subject would imitate or attempt to copy something already existing. Rather, for Adorno, mimesis involves affinity with an object. This alteration in the meaning of mimesis – or, indeed, this restoration of an older sense of mimesis – involves the abolition of a hierarchy between subject and object in which subjective reason dominates the object (Jay in Huhn and Zuidervaart 1997: 32). Such a hierarchy of subject and object is still operative when mimesis is thought of as the subject's attempt to copy something already existing. Instead, in Adorno and Horkheimer's conception of mimesis, the boundary between subject and object is permeable.

Adorno and Horkheimer explore the opposition between mimesis and enlightened reason. Instrumental reason would wish to separate itself from mimesis in order to establish its own sovereign, impermeable realm. This is nicely illustrated by the commentator Tom Huhn's recollection of the remark by the founder of psychoanalysis Sigmund Freud (1856–1939) that the development of civilization might be charted according to increases in the use of soap. According to Huhn, Freud means by this that as civilization progresses the fear of what cannot be tolerated by it – for example, dirt – is all the more acute. Soap is meant to help preserve the self from harbouring whatever might stick to it – and get into it – from outside (Huhn in Huhn 2004: 10). This is not simply the manifesto against bathing of an overgrown, grubby schoolboy. Soap stands here for reason's fear of – and increasingly alarmed attempt to control – everything that it cannot master.

No matter how clean it keeps itself, however, reason never fully succeeds in separating itself from mimesis. Again, this contention is central to the argument that there is a *dialectic* of enlightenment; that is, the argument that enlightenment is entwined with that from which it claims to have emancipated itself. We can see this mutual implication of myth and enlightenment in Adorno and Horkheimer's view of the precise way in which reason continues to be mimetic: 'The reason [*Ratio*] that represses mimesis is not merely its opposite. It is itself mimesis: of death. The subjective mind which disintegrates the spiritualization of nature masters spiritless nature only by imitating its rigidity, disintegrating itself as animistic' (DE: 44–5 [translation modified]). The term *verdrängt* is translated as 'represses' here (in preference to 'supplants' in the earlier version by John Cumming) because it emphasizes that reason remains mimetic despite itself. However, Cumming's provision of the term that in this case Adorno and Horkheimer themselves use for 'reason' – the Latin *ratio*, instead of German *Vernunft* – is helpful because it indicates that a particular understanding of reason is at work here. The primary senses in Latin of *ratio* are of 'a reckoning, account, calculation, computation' (Smith and Lockwood 1933: 615). In thinking of reason in this way here, Adorno and Horkheimer clearly draw on the view of rationality developed by the German sociologist Max Weber (1864–1920) in his book *The Protestant Ethic and the Spirit of Capitalism* and elsewhere in his work. Weber argued that the spirit of capitalism is characterized as 'that attitude which seeks profit rationally and systematically'. Capitalism, Weber claims, is an approach to the acquisition of money in which reason is tasked with calculating the outcomes for profit and loss in any and every situation (Weber 1930: 64). For Adorno and Horkheimer, this view of reason as *ratio* implies both, first, that nature is reduced to a series of precisely calculable events and, second, that reason is made into a kind of machine, a calculator.

These implications are connected. Instrumental reason becomes inanimate precisely because it has deanimated – that is, deadened, drained of meaning – the nature that it would know by means of calculation. In order to know nature, the reason that would oppose itself to nature must become like it. Simon Jarvis has drawn out very clearly the consequences of this insistence on reason's assimilation to – that is, its mimesis of – death. First, mimesis for Adorno is not just the attempt to become like nature, but moreover 'the attempt to become like nature in order to ward off what is feared'. Second, death, inconveniently, is an aspect of nature that dominating reason simply cannot overcome. In order, then, to ward off death, reason must become like it. Self-preserving reason turns self-destructive (Jarvis 1998: 31).

For Adorno and Horkheimer, a decisive separation of enlightenment from myth, of reason from mimesis, is impossible. In fact, such a separation would not even be desirable because it would require the forgetting of the aims and objectives for which reason does indeed keep itself alive; that is, such a separation would require the severing of human reason from human nature. Reason that is enlightened about itself would have to be reconciled to the fact that it is also unavoidably natural. This idea of reconciliation, which I will discuss in greater detail in later chapters, already suggests that there is something like an ethical dimension to Adorno and Horkheimer's critique of modern rationality. Reason is in conflict with nature. This conflict must, for Adorno and Horkheimer, be overcome by reconciliation rather than by reason's ultimate victory over nature. Indeed, the self-proclaimed moral neutrality of thinking which has become merely technical is not to be taken at face value. It can be shown that this pretence to neutrality has ethical presuppositions and consequences itself.

Adorno and Horkheimer, however, are far from issuing a blanket decree condemning modern rational thought as such. Moreover, they do not automatically ascribe a positive value to whatever modern rationality has suppressed. Despite the appearance that their criticisms of the course so far taken by modern rationality might suggest support for the mythic thinking from which enlightenment had supposed itself free, such a return to myth cannot be advocated by Adorno and Horkheimer for two connected reasons. First, neither enlightenment nor myth can be understood without reference to the other. On the one hand, enlightenment defines itself in opposition to myth, which, on the other hand, would not itself appear to be myth were it not distinguished from enlightenment.

Second, domination divested of its enlightened appearance is no better for having been exposed as sheer domination. Enlightened reason may not immediately appear to dominate nature – including human nature – but what went before were, precisely, attempts at direct domination. Naked power, despite its lack of dissimulation, is still only a 'dubious nobility' (DE: 37). That is, those who exercise domination over others and over nature without pretending to be enlightened are hardly to be congratulated for being cheerfully honest about what they are up to.

By guarding against any positive evaluation of unenlightened and unashamed power, Adorno and Horkheimer attempt to differentiate their position from that of certain types of interpreter of the philosopher Friedrich Nietzsche (1844–1900) who focus on his celebrations of aristocratic power as a kind of proto-fascistic celebration of the violent expression of strength. On the one hand, this kind of interpretation overlooks Nietzsche's own 'ambivalent' attitude to enlightenment, according to which both enlightenment and power are deeply implicated in the way that Adorno and Horkheimer's description of the dialectic of enlightenment sets out more fully. On the other hand, such a position is merely 'a blind eulogy of blind life' (DE: 36). (I will discuss Adorno's very interesting account of the meaning – and meaninglessness – of 'life' in Chapter 5.) What Adorno and Horkheimer are suggesting here is that quasi-fascistic appropriations of Nietzsche simply enthrone the exercise and furtherance of 'life' as an ultimate value without really questioning what life is and what meaning might be ascribed to it. As a response to the dialectic of enlightenment, nostalgia for a simpler time of the straightforward exercise of power by the strong over the weak underestimates the extent of the implication of myth and enlightenment.

DIALECTIC AND THE AIM OF CRITICAL THINKING

For such an apparently polemical book, Adorno and Horkheimer frustrate attempts to decide whether they are simply for or against enlightenment. There are two main reasons for this. First, Adorno and Horkheimer do not seek to oppose one set of apparently fixed dogmas from the perspective of a second set. Rather, they seek to begin from the given situation that enlightenment aims to overcome fear but that the world remains in the grip of fear and, furthermore, to explore what must be the case for this set of circumstances to have arisen. In order to carry out this exploration, they aim to take as seriously as possible enlightenment's own claims about itself. Second, we can come closer to grasping the procedure of *Dialectic of Enlightenment* by thinking of its authors as enemies of enlightenment for the sake of enlightenment, just as, in Adorno's phrase from his late *Negative Dialectics* (1966), 'Marx and Engels were enemies of Utopia for the sake of its realization' (ND: 322) . (Karl Marx (1818–83) and Friedrich Engels (1820–95) were the joint authors of *The Communist Manifesto* (1848) and of many other works, both together and individually.) This impressive and compact formula means that Marx and Engels were suspicious of cheery declarations that Utopia has arrived because such declarations often distract from the fact that a truly just society has not come about. Similarly, Adorno and Horkheimer are suspicious of bold proclamations that the aims of progressive thought and action have been achieved – that the world is genuinely enlightened, that reason and nature have been reconciled – because it is easier to issue such proclamations than to fulfil the aims of progressive thought. Rather than doggedly affirming the aims and achievements of enlightenment, Adorno and Horkheimer seek to re-enable enlightenment to reflect upon itself. When they draw attention to the way in which self-reflection has been aborted in enlightenment, the emphasis is on the fact that this is in contradiction with enlightenment as such. *Dialectic of Enlightenment* attempts to kick-start enlightenment's self-consciousness lest criticism of enlightenment is left to its genuine enemies.

In 1969, Adorno and Horkheimer wrote the preface to a new edition of *Dialectic of Enlightenment*. They confirm that many of the ideas put forward in the book continue to inform their work and, even more importantly, that they continue to believe that those ideas are 'timely now' (DE: xi). No such continued relevance could merely have been assumed by authors who take truth not to be invariant – that is, not to be established for all time – but who see truth as historical. But why, even if they do hold truth to be historical, should Adorno and Horkheimer feel the need to express that commitment here? After all, if *Dialectic of Enlightenment* seeks to expose what is allegedly most modern as having already prevailed for millennia, then is there really any hope that there would have been a genuine change in the twenty-two years from 1947, when the book was first published, to 1969, the year of the new edition? This question touches upon an apparent contradiction in *Dialectic of Enlightenment*. On the one hand, Adorno and Horkheimer hold that 'the newest ideologies are a mere reprise of the oldest' (DE: 42). On the other, such a conclusion seems to be vigorously disavowed because it partakes in the hardening of enlightened rigour into mythic fate:

> The arid wisdom which acknowledges nothing new under the sun, because all the pieces in the meaningless game have been played out, all the great thoughts have been thought, all possible discoveries can be construed in advance, and human beings are defined by self-preservation through adaptation – this barren wisdom merely reproduces the fantastic doctrine it rejects: the sanction of fate which, through retribution, incessantly reinstates what always was. Whatever might be different is the same. That is the verdict which critically sets the boundaries to possible experience.
>
> (DE: 8)

This looks like a contradiction. Adorno and Horkheimer reject the view that there is nothing new under the sun as 'arid wisdom' but later go on to state that new ideologies are just the same as the old ones. On the one hand, they criticize the rejection of the possibility of newness, whereas, on the other, they declare that something which appears new is, in fact, old.

What prevents such a position from being fatally caught on the horns of the dilemma that it faces is Adorno and Horkheimer's concern not just with diagnosing what has always been the case but with trying to allow space for what might yet be possible. The phrase 'the boundaries to possible experience' in the above passage is revealing. Setting limits to possible experience, according to Adorno and Horkheimer, tacitly sets up the world as it is and always has been so far as the only possible world. On the contrary, Adorno and Horkheimer view the limits of experience not as handed down from heaven but as historically formed and hence changeable. The limits of experience are not, therefore, necessarily binding for ever. This argument is, of course, as much about the world as it is about experience. As with their view of experience, that is, Adorno and Horkheimer are just as suspicious of any view that ultimately shrugs and concedes 'that's the way of the world'. For sure, only certain types of experience have *so far* been possible and only a certain type of world has *so far* existed. Adorno and Horkheimer aim to hold open the possibility that there might be different experiences and a different world. They refuse to accept that what has been the case up to now is what must always be the case. This is not to say that Adorno and Horkheimer suggest that all we have to do is wait for some rapturous apocalyptic moment when the possibilities for new experience will be unleashed and when the world will no longer be ordered just as it always has been. Vigilance is required. Adorno and Horkheimer are suspicious of any declaration that something genuinely new is immediately on offer. There is a difference between something that is genuinely a departure from what has always been the case and something that simply claims to be new but is in fact old, dressed up in the garb of mere novelty. This vigilance is characteristic of Adorno's critique of what he and Horkheimer called the 'culture industry'. I will explore this critique in the next chapter.

SUMMARY

In *Dialectic of Enlightenment*, Adorno and Horkheimer ask how successfully enlightened thought has freed itself from myth. They see crucial aspects of enlightenment – the reduction of nature to mere matter and the unavoidable deathliness of reason that goes with it – as unenlightened aspects of enlightened reason. The aim of *Dialectic of Enlightenment* is not to overthrow enlightenment in a debauched return to the open expression of strength, but rather to reinitiate enlightenment's reflection on itself. Adorno and Horkheimer wish to suggest that limits to possible experience are limits to the kind of experience that has so far been historically possible: the possibility of new experience and of a new world is held open.

2

FUN

We have been concerned in the first chapter of this book with the central arguments of *Dialectic of Enlightenment*. Adorno and Horkheimer contend that reason aims to liberate humanity from the fear of nature. This aim to go beyond the mythic fear and ignorance of nature is 'enlightenment'. The way that reason has so far set about trying to achieve this aim is by reducing nature to the inert and meaningless object of rational domination. Reason itself is affected by this. First, reason has, in setting up the hard and false division between itself and nature, forgotten that it is in some senses also natural. Second, reason has become inert, like the nature that it dominates. Enlightenment is not as finally distinct from myth as enlightenment would like to make out. In this way, it is 'dialectical'. Adorno and Horkheimer do not suggest, however, that the project of enlightenment should simply be written off as a disastrous experiment. Enlightenment resulting in rational domination of nature is incomplete enlightenment. What is required is the completion of enlightenment, the achievement of its fundamental aims, so that human nature may be fully reconciled with itself and with non-human nature.

This brief recapitulation of *Dialectic of Enlightenment* is important because the arguments developed in it are central to Adorno's account of what he and Horkheimer called the 'culture industry'. At first sight, the inclusion of a chapter on the radio, films and magazines of mid-twentieth-century America can seem odd in a book about the history of rationality from animism (the belief that objects are inhabited by spirits) to logical positivism (the twentieth-century philosophical position, associated chiefly with A.J. Ayer (1910–89), according to which statements that are not verifiable are simply meaningless). Adorno and Horkheimer acknowledge – in what has seemed to some the aloof tone that marks all of Adorno's cultural theory – that the products of the culture industry are granted more importance than they inherently demand. But the point of discussing the Lone Ranger's trousers, astrology columns and Donald Duck is to show that the standardization wrought on nature has even been extended to those areas of life that are presented as having slipped through the net of rationalization. Moreover, it is not just that Adorno seeks to show that the culture industry remains implicated in the workaday world from which it supposedly offers respite. Rather, the culture industry is meant to foster adaptation, on the part of the consumers of its products, to the world as it is currently configured.

This chapter's main focus is on Adorno's argument that the culture industry dissolves both its own products and the possibility of anything like a meaningful response to them on the part of its consumers. The products of the culture industry consist – if, indeed, 'consist' is the right word – in a series of parts strung together without relation to a whole. Any cinematic blockbuster is just about the scene where the expensive special effects are shown off to best effect. You can forget the rest of the film but don't forget how much that explosion would have cost. The product of the culture industry, according to Adorno, is not a 'work' and, in this and a number of related senses, it is not art. This kind of product aims to elicit a particular response in its consumers, who, as consumers, are already restricted to certain responses. Indeed, its sole aim is to produce an effect – titillation, shock, awe – rather than to have significance in itself. But this kind of response is not, Adorno suggests, really a response in any meaningful way. Indeed, fun is stupid, but it turns out not even to be all that much fun. Finally, I will look briefly in this chapter at some possible criticisms of Adorno's view of culture, focusing in particular on his alleged elitism and underestimation of the products of the culture industry.

INDUSTRY AND CULTURE

Hollywood is bad for the environment. A recent report by the University of California at Los Angeles found that the amount of carbon dioxide emitted by film studios in Los Angeles is second only to the amount emitted by the region's oil refineries. Mary Nichols, head of UCLA's Institute of the

Environment and one of the report's authors, offered the following account of the idea behind the report: 'People talk of "the industry", but we don't think of them as an industry. We think of the creative side, the movie, the people, the actors – we don't think of what it takes to produce the product' (Glaister 2006: 19). What exactly 'industry' means in the phrase 'culture industry' needs to be specified because it has for Adorno both the literal sense that contemporary cultural products are often manufactured by technological means, and the broader and more significant sense that cultural products rely on a particular system of distribution. For Adorno, it is significant both that the culture industry is happy to refer to itself in this kind of way and that the real significance of describing culture as an industry has been forgotten. Adorno discusses the meaning of 'industry' in this context in the essay in which he reflects on the account of the culture industry developed in *Dialectic of Enlightenment*, 'Culture Industry Reconsidered'. He remarks that 'the expression "industry" is not to be taken too literally' because what is more significant than the techniques deployed in the manufacture of films, magazines and so on is how these products function in society (CI: 100–1). The term 'industry' is intended 'more in a sociological sense' than in a strictly technical sense. What is crucial is the way in which cultural products have been standardized and distributed by means of rationalized and strictly controlled organization.

While this kind of account of the meaning of 'industry' in the phrase 'culture industry' allows us to grasp more firmly what Adorno intended by this expression, its full meaning begins to come fully into view only when we consider how Adorno and Horkheimer might otherwise have designated what they call the 'culture industry' in *Dialectic of Enlightenment*. Again, Adorno reflects on this in 'Culture Industry Reconsidered', which begins with an account of why other ways of describing cultural products consumed on a large scale are to be shunned. He notes that he and Horkheimer avoided terms like 'mass culture' and 'popular culture' because they do not properly describe what they label and because, Adorno implies, they therefore participate in the culture industry's favourable portrayal of itself. For Adorno, the culture industry is emphatically not 'a matter of something like a culture that arises spontaneously from the masses themselves, the contemporary form of popular art' (CI: 98). This statement has two very significant aspects. First, the culture industry is not 'popular' in that its products are only consumed – and not produced – by 'the people'. It is not, according to Adorno, a sufficient condition of 'popular culture' that 'the people' consume it. Importantly, Adorno explicitly separates the culture industry from popular art, which therefore leaves open the possibility that there might be – or, more likely, might have been – art which is popular and which is, indeed, art. Second, the products of the culture industry are not spontaneously produced. This denial of spontaneity is central to Adorno's characterization of the culture industry's industrial character and thus central, moreover, to its participation in enlightened rationality's reduction of all phenomena to an unchanging substrate such as (as we saw in the last chapter) 'matter' or 'mere objectivity'. The best illustration of this denial of spontaneity is Adorno and Horkheimer's account in *Dialectic of Enlightenment* of the way in which talent is made to conform to the industry standard:

> Any trace of spontaneity in the audience of the official radio is steered and absorbed into a selection of specializations by talent-spotters, performance competitions, and sponsored events of every kind. The talents belong to the operation long before they are put on show; otherwise they would not conform so eagerly.

(DE: 96)

This control of spontaneity has only intensified since *Dialectic of Enlightenment* and the rest of Adorno's cultural theory were written. The process of the selection and processing of talent – the industrialized operation of culture – has itself become entertainment in programmes such as *The X-Factor* and *American Idol*, in which would-be music stars compete for the votes of the audience, and the competitor with the most votes secures a lucrative recording contract. With their bastardized versions of democracy – testified to in their over-earnest insistence on the determination of their outcomes by the viewers, as if the voting had been overseen by independent electoral monitors – these shows are evidence that the tendencies Adorno identified in the culture industry have become more entrenched. Indeed, the very title of *The X-Factor* testifies to the fact that any critical reflection on the products of the culture industry is to be disallowed: all the works of the culture industry are the result of a mysterious, almost supernatural 'X factor', the workings of which cannot be submitted to scrutiny. You've either got it or you haven't.

JUST ADD WATER

A picture of the culture industry according to Adorno, as well as the continued relevance of that picture to prominent aspects of contemporary cultural production, is beginning to emerge. Broadly speaking, we can say that there is one chief characteristic of the culture industry which has two significant correlates or consequences: the culture industry reduces its products to a uniform standard, which in turn entails both the dissolution of the work and the dissolution of genuine response to it. It is not just that artworks are split into a series of momentary thrills but, even more radically, that their specific character is entirely indifferent to the culture industry. The first consequence of the standardization of cultural products – the dissolution of them as works – means, therefore, that according to the culture industry, on Adorno's account, the specific quality of any film, book or television programme hardly matters; what is fundamental is that it fits into currently existing forms. Differences between cultural products have less to do with whether, for example, a particular film is a horror or a romantic comedy than with 'classifying, organizing, and labelling consumers'. The choice on offer is one between things that are the same. Adorno sets out in more detail the meaning for cultural products themselves of this relationship between pre-established forms and content:

> The concept of technique in the culture industry is only in name identical with technique in works of art. In the latter, technique is concerned with the internal organization of the object itself, with its inner logic. In contrast, the technique of the culture industry is, from the beginning, one of distribution and mechanical reproduction, and therefore always remains external to its object.
> (CI: 101)

The machinery can churn out apparently different products without the techniques of production and distribution themselves being affected in any way.

Just as the machinery of the culture industry is always ready to produce more of the same, so what is actually produced is always ready for easy consumption. The standardized goods of the culture industry are a kind of ready-meal. The culinary metaphor, which Adorno frequently uses in his cultural theory, is apt because it emphasizes that cultural products need only be consumed without further ado or effort on the part of the consumer. This central aspect of the culture industry is the focus of one of Adorno's most important and difficult essays in cultural theory, 'The Schema of Mass Culture'. When Adorno describes cultural products as 'pre-digested' he means that the response to them is already precisely anticipated by them. The instructions to a so-called 'live' studio audience to 'LAUGH NOW' and

'CLAP NOW' are only the most extreme forms of this kind of anticipation of response.

The culture industry does not facilitate real spontaneity or real choices. The appearances of spontaneity and choice are actually functions of the way in which the culture industry makes sure it has everyone in its grip. Adorno and Horkheimer again point to the system according to which products of the culture industry are categorized. The distinctions between cultural products – from genres of film to magazines in different price brackets – are not really significant in themselves, Adorno and Horkheimer argue, but are rather the means by which different people are catered for by the same mechanism: 'Something is provided for everyone so that no one can escape; differences are hammered home and propagated.' Thus, the consumer's response is already implied by the product that they consume. 'Everyone is supposed to behave spontaneously according to a "level" determined by the indices and to select the category of mass product manufactured for their type' (DE: 97). The culture industry relies on the most rigid aesthetic laws to which its consumers adhere. Everyone already knows what kind of thing they like. The response that matters is buying it.

DISSOLUTION OF THE WORK AND DISSOLUTION OF RESPONSE

I have been claiming that Adorno sees the features of the culture industry as having two main consequences: the dissolution of the work of art and the dissolution of aesthetic response. It is clear that in this way the culture industry participates in enlightened rationality's reduction of nature and deadening of its own reason because, on the one hand, its products are merely the repetition of the same thing produced repeatedly to a standardized pattern, and, on the other, response to those products is similarly standardized and foreordained. Crucially for Adorno, the products of the culture industry are not coherent 'works' for two main reasons. First, the cultural product is merely a series of parts aimed exclusively at achieving certain effects in the consumer. There is 'order, not connections' in the cultural product, which is to say that the parts, as it were, hang together, but that they relate neither to one another nor to the larger category under which they are subsumed (DE: 99). Second, the product of the culture industry – unlike art, for reasons that I will set out fully in the next chapter – remains a part of empirical existence. As a mere part, it fails to be a whole.

This aspect of the products of the culture industry – that they do not constitute successful aesthetic wholes – is perhaps the chief consequence of the fact that, unlike artworks, they are not distinct from empirical reality. Whereas art is counterpoised to reality, products of the culture industry are part of and, crucially, reinforce it. This is one of the most important claims of Adorno's cultural theory and it explains the importance that is ascribed to the culture industry both in *Dialectic of Enlightenment* and throughout Adorno's theory of culture. Indeed, as Adorno and Horkheimer point out, 'the culture industry is taken more seriously than it might itself wish to be' because it relates to contemporary reason and society in two important ways. First, the culture industry relies on the calculation of certain effects in consumers and, as we have seen, calculation is a central feature of modern *ratio*. Second, and especially significant for understanding how the culture industry relates to existence, the culture industry is shown not to separate itself from existence in the way that art does but rather as engaging in 'the idolization of the existing order' (DE: xix). While the culture industry poses as an escape or rest from the rigours of contemporary existence, any difference between it and the world as it is constituted at present is, in fact, merely superficial. 'On all sides,' claims Adorno, 'the borderline between culture and empirical reality becomes more and more indistinct' (CI: 61). Tabloid reporting of the fisticuffs and extra-marital shenanigans of soap-opera characters as if they were real events would not be mere eccentricities from Adorno's perspective but the fulfilled logic of the culture industry's relationship to existing reality.

Both the dissolution of the work and the dissolution of response are treated in one of Adorno's earliest accounts of the culture industry, 'On the Fetish Character in Music and the Regression of Listening'. Before I look at the central arguments of this essay, we need to attend, first, to its title and, second, to the background of Adorno's involvement with American academic sociology, against which it was written. First, what do the terms 'fetish' and 'regression' mean? The fact that these terms are taken from Marx and Freud, respectively, indicates the importance of these thinkers – and of the combination of their thought – to Adorno's work. 'Fetish' is deployed early on in Marx's *Capital* (first volume, 1867; second and third volumes published posthumously, 1885 and 1894) to describe the 'mysterious character' of the commodity-form (Marx 1976: 164). Marx contests that through exchange, products of labour take on an exchange-value distinct from their value as utilizable objects. A commodity, then, is intended not solely for use but for exchange. Marx states that exchange-value is 'socially uniform', which is to say that in the process of exchange, different things are treated as equivalent. This social uniformity of exchange-value contrasts with 'sensuously varied' use-value; that is, with the specific differences in the way that actually different things are used (Marx 1976: 166). Thus, the computer on which I am writing this cost about the same as my smart suit: their exchange-value is equivalent but their use-value is different. Although it is entirely produced by human labour and although exchange depends entirely on social relations between human beings, the specific characteristics of the commodity come to appear objective; that is, they appear to be qualities of the thing itself, rather than the results of certain social processes. This appearance, of course, is false. 'So far,' Marx states, 'no chemist has ever discovered exchange-value either in a pearl or a diamond' (Marx 1976: 177). No branch of the physical sciences can point to the exchange-value of anything because, quite simply, it does not exist; that human actions and processes have taken on lives of their own that human beings think they do not control is the fetishism of the commodity. The particular aspects of commodity fetishism that Adorno emphasizes in his essay on the fetish-character of music are, on the one hand, the fact that hit songs are produced as much for the money they will make – the crucial marker of success in the culture industry – as for the quality of their music, and, on the other hand, the fact that listeners to hit songs adopt a passive, unthinking role, allowing the commodified music apparently to lead a life of its own. Marx's concept of fetishism, then, is central to Adorno's view of how the music of the culture industry implies the dissolution of the work and the dissolution of response to it.

Dissolution of adequate response is central to Adorno's understanding of 'regression' as well. The idea of 'regression' is taken from Freud, who first discussed this idea extensively in *The Interpretation of Dreams* (1899), in which he characterized it as a kind of psychological reversal. Regression occurs in a dream when 'an idea is turned back into the sensory image from which it is derived' (Freud 1976: 693). To put this another way, regression occurs when a thought's progress into a higher psychological stage is somehow blocked or opposed. Importantly, Freud did not confine the idea of regression to the interpretation of dreams, but rather held it also to be central to neuroses and mental illnesses. Thus mental illness is ultimately, for Freud, a return to earlier, primitive stages of pre-mental functioning. (This is not to say (for Adorno if not for Freud) that in order to overcome regression we must simply grow up: fully achieved maturity would have to realize the child's wish for happiness ever after, not scorn it from the perspective of an all-too-knowing world-weariness.) It is important to note here that Adorno is not especially interested in psychoanalysis as a kind of therapy, as 'a technique of psychological massage' (PMP: 96). His interest in Freud has to do with what psychoanalysis can tell us about society, especially with regard to what society has made of the individuals who comprise it. Moreover, Adorno's view of Freud's significance for the consideration of society is distinctive because it does not locate his importance for social critique exclusively in his more recognizably socio-critical works, such as, for example, *Civilization and Its Discontents* (1930). While Adorno is certainly interested in this aspect of Freud's authorship, he also reads Freud's more strictly psychological works as, at the same time, records pertaining as much to society as to the psychology of the isolated individual.

This consideration of the terms of the title of 'On the Fetish Character in Music and the Regression of Listening' has enabled me briefly to discuss some very important influences on Adorno's thinking. It is also worth setting 'On the Fetish Character' in the context of the stage of Adorno's professional life to which it belongs. This essay was the first that he wrote during his exile in America. As a way to strengthen the connections between the Institute for Social Research and American academic sociology, as well as to secure a position for Adorno in America despite the institute's increasingly straitened financial situation, Horkheimer arranged for Adorno to work with the American sociologist Paul Lazarsfeld (1901–76) on a project to investigate the social impact of radio. While Adorno's experiences working under Lazarsfeld are important for the development of his conception of sociology, it was clear that Adorno's background in music criticism and philosophy did not sit comfortably with the radio research project as Lazarsfeld had envisaged it from the perspective of his more empirical approach to social research. In particular, Adorno was resistant to the need to collect quantifiable results by means of questionnaires following a standard pattern, rather than, as Adorno preferred, a focus on the qualitative impact of radio on music and its reception as such (Müller-Doohm 2005: 246–51). One result of Adorno's frustration with the project associated with Lazarsfeld was his own attempt to consider more philosophically the impact of the industrialization of modern music intended for mass consumption.

Central to the argument of 'On the Fetish Character' is the claim that industrial cultural products are not artworks because their constitutive parts do not add up, or relate, to a whole. Rather, a hit song is merely, Adorno contests, a series of isolated bits:

The delight in the moment and the gay façade becomes an excuse for absolving the listener from the thought of the whole, whose claim is comprised in proper listening. The listener is converted, along his line of least resistance, into the acquiescent purchaser. No longer do the partial moments serve as critique of that whole; instead, they suspend the critique which the successful aesthetic totality exerts against the flawed one of society. The unitary synthesis is sacrificed to them; they no longer produce their own in place of the reified one, but show themselves complaisant to it. The isolated moments of enjoyment prove incompatible with the immanent constitution of the work of art, and whatever in the work goes beyond them to an essential perception is sacrificed to them. They are not bad in themselves but in their diversionary function.

(CI: 32–3)

We need to attend closely to the detail of this passage – and, importantly, to the development of its argument – because it contains some of the most important aspects of Adorno's critique of contemporary cultural products. In particular, the passage as a whole is framed by statements in its opening and closing sentences regarding the relationship between pleasure and thought. This relationship is fundamental not just to Adorno's cultural and aesthetic theory but to his whole conception of thinking and intellectual labour.

The opening sentence of this passage asserts that, as merely a series of isolated moments, contemporary hit songs substitute the *enjoyment* of jaunty effects for the *thought* of the significance of the whole. Adorno implies that pleasure – or at least the type of pleasure in which the culture industry deals – attaches itself to isolated moments, whereas thought necessarily proceeds beyond mere moments to consider the entirety of which such parts are, indeed, parts. A more or less straightforward opposition between pleasure and thought seems to be the result, then, of the opening sentence of this passage.

In the products of the culture industry – here, hit songs – delight becomes 'an excuse for absolving the listener from the thought of the whole' (CI: 32). However, this conclusion is significantly qualified in a number of ways that have often been overlooked or downplayed in much of the commentary on Adorno's account of the culture industry in particular and on his aesthetic theory more generally. The final sentence of the passage states that it is not, in fact, that moments of pleasure are bad as such. Rather, they are bad in that they divert attention away from thought. Isolated moments of pleasure are bad, first, in that they separate isolated moments from a whole of which they would be parts and, second, in that pleasure replaces or blocks thought. The implication is that pleasure is *not necessarily* opposed to thinking. Moreover, Adorno also strongly intimates in a number of places not only that pleasure detached from thought is inadequate because it is unthinking but that such pleasure is not really pleasure at all. It is as if the moments of pleasure are suffocated by the mediocre cushioning with which they are surrounded: 'In isolation, the charms become dulled and furnish models of the familiar' (CI: 33). Real delight is swapped for familiarity. Adorno claims at the beginning of 'On the Fetish Character' that liking and disliking are no longer appropriate to the products of the culture industry: 'The familiarity of the piece is a surrogate for the quality ascribed to it. To like it is almost the same thing as to recognize it' (CI: 30).

It is important to understand a statement like this – that genuine liking has been swapped for mere familiarity – in the context of Adorno's reception of philosophical aesthetics. Kant's *Critique of the Power of Judgement* (1790; often also known in English as *Critique of Judgement*) has a fairly strong claim to having established the tradition of modern philosophical aesthetics. Certain prominent features of Kant's aesthetics are very much behind Adorno's discussion of the relationship between taste and familiarity. Kant argued that aesthetic response was to be conceived as the special ability of a distinct faculty or capacity of taste. Judgements of taste, for Kant, are autonomous. This means that they are to be carefully separated from different types of judgement – including judgements that yield knowledge, moral judgements, and judgements about what simply makes me feel good – in order to secure for themselves their own special area of competence. Taste is grounded, for Kant, on a liking or disliking that does not refer to what something is, what it can teach us morally, or how it merely moves me in some less dignified and more pathological way. Adorno was both profoundly indebted to Kant's account of taste and insightfully critical of some of its fundamental assumptions.

Adorno's criticisms of the *Critique of the Power of Judgement* will be examined in the next chapter. It is necessary here to attend to the exact significance of Adorno's statement that taste is 'outmoded' and that it has been replaced by familiarity. Taste is 'outmoded' because the kind of autonomy which Kant held to be fundamental to taste is no longer possible. This view does not necessarily imply a criticism of Kant's theory of taste. This is the case for two connected reasons. First, Kant himself established the opposition between taste and familiarity. For Kant, if I make a judgement based on the fact, for example, that this song is an example of the kind of music that I know I like, or that I have to like this song in order to fit in, then such a judgement is not a judgement of taste. In fact, as the French literary theorist and philosophical aesthetician Gérard Genette has usefully made clear, this would really be, for Kant, a feigned judgement and not, for that reason, a proper judgement at all (Genette 1999: 197). Second, Adorno emphasizes not that taste is a bad thing – in a way similar to his statement that isolated moments of pleasure are not bad in themselves – but rather that the freedom of choice and contemplative detachment required for it are no longer possible in contemporary circumstances.

FREE TIME

Adorno's suspicion of how freely consumers of cultural products make choices is echoed by his suspicion of the freedom of the 'free time' that people spend consuming them. Cultural products are standardized in such a way that they require only the most stultified response. Where cultural products repeat and re-enforce the empirical world as it is, fun and free time in general, according to Adorno, actually prolong the duress of work for which they are supposed to compensate. We need to concentrate on this claim here – that free time is an extension of work – and to consider how it fits into Adorno's characterization of the kinds of modes of response elicited by the culture industry more generally.

To begin with, the claim that fun is like work seems quite simply to contradict the claim that fun is detached from conceptual labour, from the work of thinking, and is therefore inadequate. Adorno, however, does not shy away from this contradiction. Rather, the contradiction that fun both be like work and that it not involve any thought is one that Adorno views as prevailing in the contemporary mode of free time itself. In his essay 'Free Time' he comments on this problem:

It is widely known but no less true therefore that specific leisure activities like tourism and camping revolve around and are organised for the sake of profit. At the same time the difference between work and free time has been branded as a norm in the minds of people, at both the conscious and unconscious level. Because, in accordance with the predominant work ethic, time free of work should be utilized for the recreation of expended labour power, then work-less time, precisely because it is a mere appendage to work, is severed from the latter with puritanical zeal.

(CI: 189)

Because free time is to function as the renewal of the ability to work, it must not, therefore, contain work. This is why it is so important to 'switch off' and to 'recharge your batteries'. Work and pleasure are both damaged when the relationship between them is configured in this way. Work is to be taken absolutely seriously; enjoyment of work is accidental to it. Enjoyment, precisely because it must allow for the recreation of labour power, must not expend the kinds of energy required for work.

The basic function of free time in contemporary society is well summarized by one of the pieces of advice that Adorno quotes in his study of the *Los Angeles Times* astrology column, 'The Stars Down to Earth': 'TAURUS: Attend to essential home duties early; then venture forth and make yourself more charming by means of beauty treatments, haircuts, dieting. In P.M. have fun; be happy' (SDE: 65). The seriousness of the morning's activities is reinforced in this itinerary by a kind of heroic rhetoric: paying the bills and fixing the guttering are 'duties' solemnly to be conducted before you 'venture forth'. Moreover, fun and happiness, despite – or, rather, because of – their juxtaposition with the rigours of the morning, are made to seem compulsory. Fun is a duty as well. Adorno's account of free time attempts to show how, in separating joyful indulgence from serious work, the part of the schedule set aside for fun never yields what it promises. This timetabling of fun is implicitly taken as evidence for Adorno and Horkheimer's thesis that the rational self is based on the renunciation of the immediate satisfaction of impulse. The separation of indulgence from reason – its confinement to a discrete slot in the schedule – is not an essential feature of indulgence. While the timetable allows equal slots to reason and fun, rationalization ultimately prevails because the drawing up of a timetable is itself a demand of rationality.

A set of important claims regarding the relationship between reason and its other in rationalized society is beginning to emerge. I discussed in the last chapter how Adorno and Horkheimer attempted to show, in a way which developed elements of Weber's analysis of capitalistic rationality, that reason fixated on self-preservation becomes self-destructive. Likewise, Adorno again adopts a thought of Weber's in the context of his discussion of the culture industry: it is not necessarily the case that irrational elements are in conflict with society's overall rationality; rather, it is perfectly possible for a rationalized society to pursue irrational ends (Weber 1930: 77–8). That is, phenomena or modes of behaviour that appear to be irrational are, in fact, examples of 'the processes of rational self preservation "run amuck"' (SDE: 47).

This perverted rationality is fundamental to the connection between the culture industry and adaptation to prevailing circumstances. Adorno most clearly establishes this connection in his account of what rationality has come to mean in the astrology column of the *Los Angeles Times*. The source in the stars of the information presented in the column is kept opaque. Indeed, this is where the irrationality of astrology rests for Adorno: while the movements of the stars and humdrum personal advice are rational enough, combining them is not. No explanation is offered as to why the movements of the stars make Tuesday a good day for settling disputes with colleagues. For Adorno, this opaqueness of the reasoning behind the astrology column provides an important clue to its social function. Like astrology, society is opaque and inscrutable, in the sense that most people simply do not grasp how it works, and even to those who do attempt to understand society it is not amenable to fully adequate rational explanation. Adorno comments that it is more tempting simply to accept this absurdity rather than to engage in the painful process of penetrating it through thinking (SDE: 57). The astrology column counsels on behalf of existing reality that if you want to get on in life, it is more 'rational' just to accept your lot than to try to think about it too hard because, if you did that, you wouldn't get very far anyway. Adaptation is necessarily also acceptance. Adorno and Horkheimer reinforce this point in their account of the kind of pleasure advanced by the culture industry. Entertainment is necessarily affirmative because the escape offered by it is not escape from a bad reality at all but rather escape from the very idea of resistance to that reality (DE: 115). The only way out is surrender.

ADORNO'S ELITISM?

Adorno's cultural theory inevitably provokes a number of objections. One of the most prominent to his account of cultural products – cinematic blockbusters, astrology, advertising and so on – is that his view seems to assume that the consumers of such products are stupid; that is, that they are wholly incapable of seeing through what he casts as the swindle perpetrated on them. However, as the famous closing sentence of the chapter on the culture industry in *Dialectic of Enlightenment* makes clear, Adorno thinks that people *do* see through the products of the culture industry, but that they do this while nevertheless consuming them (DE: 136). How is it possible to be swindled and to recognize the swindle at the same time, according to Adorno? As J.M. Bernstein has shown in his trenchant defence of Adorno's cultural theory against the postmodern advocacy of 'popular culture', the culture industry does not demand, according to Adorno, strict adherence or belief in order to succeed in its aim of being consumed (CI: 1–28). Rather, as Adorno made clear in his account of astrology in particular, the irrationality and coercion of the culture industry are kept at arm's length. Adorno's response to the objection that his theory assumes the stupidity of the consumers of cultural products is one of the most important – and perhaps most pessimistic – aspects of his thinking. It is important because it echoes Adorno's broader insistence that real faults with the state of the world will not be solved simply by recognizing them as such. It is pessimistic, therefore, because righting those wrongs is going to be much harder than we thought.

It is unlikely that the rehearsal of this objection and of Adorno's response to it will entirely satisfy defenders of contemporary mass culture. While the consumers might be thought to be off the hook in that they don't actually believe in the products of the culture industry, Adorno still thinks that those products are rubbish. His critique is not directed uniformly, however, against every example of mass culture. For example, in his essay 'How to Look at Television', Adorno remarks that the early culture industry of the eighteenth and nineteenth centuries in fact fostered certain types of innovation: 'When the journalist Defoe and the printer Richardson calculated the effect of their wares upon the audience, they had to speculate, to follow hunches; and therewith, a certain latitude to develop deviations remained' (CI: 160–1). The important term here is 'speculate'. With writers like Daniel Defoe (1660–1731) and Samuel Richardson (1689–1761) – whose backgrounds were in trades (journalism and printing, respectively) rather than in art – this term had certainly started to mean the investment of money in order to accumulate more money. But it also still meant for Defoe and Richardson, Adorno suggests, the freedom to deviate from established norms and to experiment regardless of an expected outcome. Adorno goes on to remark that in novels produced and consumed on a large scale in the early nineteenth century, about a hundred years after Defoe's enormously influential *Robinson Crusoe* (published 1719), and fifty or so after the huge success of Richardson's didactic tales *Pamela* and *Clarissa* (1740–1 and 1747–8, respectively), the way in which the great multitudes of plots and sub-plots were developed within novels allowed for a certain openness of expectation in readers. It is not the case for Adorno, therefore, that the culture industry represents the contemporary form of popular art as such. His critique of culture is not aimed at anything that could be conceived of as the essential set of characteristics of mass-produced art for mass consumption. As we saw in his discussion of isolated moments of delight in contemporary music, it is not that cultural products are bad in themselves. What Adorno objects to in contemporary culture is precisely the failure of cultural products to fulfil their own potential. This failure is a consequence of the fact that that potential is sacrificed because everything must fit into existing moulds. For Adorno, these characteristics are not shared by art, and it is to his theory of art that we must now turn.

SUMMARY

Adorno refuses to see the 'culture industry' as the contemporary form of 'popular art': that culture is consumed by 'the people' is insufficient for it to be designated as genuinely 'popular'. He claims that the products of the culture industry are debased and that they foster unthinking and passive response. Indeed, this kind of response is already programmed, as it were, into films, pulp fiction, magazines and so on. A central part of Adorno's theory of contemporary culture is aimed at questioning the division between work and leisure, or 'free time'. The latter, Adorno contends, is very much an extension of work, even where its difference from work is energetically championed. Adorno defends his theory of culture from the charge that it assumes the stupidity of its consumers through recourse to an account of how a rational society can still serve irrational ends.

3

ART

IS ART SERIOUS?

As I showed in the last chapter, Adorno's critique of the culture industry is
in part based on a suspicion of how much fun 'fun' really is. The pleasures
to which the culture industry is dedicated are hollowed out, devoid of any
really substantial satisfaction. Crucial to this view is the judgement that they
are unthinking pleasures. Adorno argues that one of the most important
conditions of the possibility of the culture industry is the careful policing of
a rigid border between unreflective consumption and attentive reflection.
Therefore, for these reasons among others, the culture industry is to be
radically distinguished from art. Does this mean, then, that whereas the
culture industry purveys a kind of dreary fun, art is serious? At first sight,
Adorno's aesthetics can appear as an unrelenting insistence on the seriousness
of art. We would be wrong to attempt to dilute this insistence by making the
consideration of art in Adorno's work conform to a more recognizable and
innocuous model. Art does have an unusually privileged status in Adorno's
thinking. It is worth considering in this connection, however, a set of
Adorno's reflections on the question, 'Is art lighthearted?' included in *Notes
to Literature*. In these reflections, Adorno responds to a line from the poet and
philosopher Friedrich von Schiller (1759–1805): 'Life is serious, art is
lighthearted'. While we might expect Adorno simply to rebuff a statement
such as this with an account of the seriousness of art, instead he seeks again

to question the rigid opposition between pleasure and thought. Art is not exclusively to be categorized as either serious or lighthearted. On the one hand, art has escaped the deadening rule of seriousness that prevails in reality – the seriousness which constantly exhorts that it's a hard life in the real world – because art cannot be thought of as a part of reality in any straightforward way. To this extent, art is lighthearted. On the other hand, and again for the reason that it has escaped reality, art suggests a change in consciousness, which is to say that it contains the suggestion that it might be possible for a different kind of reality to exist. In this way, art is serious. 'As something that has escaped from reality and is nevertheless permeated with it,' Adorno states, 'art vibrates between this seriousness and light-heartedness. It is this tension that constitutes art' (NL II: 249). This is a crucial definition of art, not only because it remains true to Adorno's criticism of the distinction between work and pleasure, but because it reveals one of the most important aspects of art in Adorno's view. Art is both real and separate from reality, which is to say, more specifically, that art is both social and that it is critical of society. Care is needed here because, on the one hand, the social nature of any artwork is not straightforwardly to be garnered from the social context of its production, while, on the other, artworks do not criticize society simply by containing within them straightforward expressions of opinions. Introducing Adorno's theory of the way in which artworks are both social and critical of society without simply being reduced to what they explicitly declare is one of the main tasks of this chapter. His view of the socially critical status of art is closely associated with his claim that art can have what he calls a 'truth-content'. Again, care is needed when considering this term because artworks are not more or less true by virtue of being more or less packed full of verifiable philosophical propositions. Adorno's conception of what it means for art in some way to be 'true' is equally central to this chapter.

It is worth noting at the outset that Adorno's aesthetic theory does not fit comfortably into the academically established category of 'aesthetics' as a sub-discipline of philosophy. Indeed, for Adorno art and aesthetic experience are not adequately treated when they are considered according to the criteria of aesthetics as it is usually conceived. Rather, reflection on art is, for Adorno, ethical, metaphysical and logical, as well as aesthetic in the immediately recognizable sense of that term. As is well known, had Adorno lived to complete *Aesthetic Theory*, he planned to choose as its epigraph a 'Critical Fragment' from the German Romantic philosopher Friedrich von Schlegel (1772–1829): 'What one calls philosophy of art usually lacks one of two things: either the philosophy or the art' (Schlegel 1967: 148 [my translation]). It is important to emphasize the fact that Adorno would have chosen this remark of Schlegel's as the epigraph to *Aesthetic Theory*. It is not just that in *Aesthetic Theory* Adorno attempted to supplement a richly art-historical account with philosophical rigour, or vice versa. Rather, what Adorno wants to argue is that art is in a very significant way itself philo-sophical and, perhaps still more intriguingly, that philosophy is itself artistic. The first of these ideas is central here; I will explore the second more fully at the beginning of the next chapter.

AESTHETIC AUTONOMY AND THE TRUTH OF ART

There has not always been such a thing as art. The altarpiece that hangs in the gallery and the cantatas performed in the concert hall were not always 'art' in the way that we have come to understand it. The contemporary Italian philosopher Giorgio Agamben (b. 1942) has provided a detailed account of how our notions of art and aesthetic judgement differ radically from earlier views. In *The Man without Content*, Agamben gives the example of the late medieval practice among the wealthy and learned of collecting and displaying an array of unusual objects in a *Wunderkammer*, or 'cabinet of wonder'. The cabinet would have contained objects that we might now want to classify as 'art' alongside objects it would not occur to us to classify in this way. For the medieval scholar, Agamben argues, the 'cabinet of wonder' was a miniature universe in which 'the individual objects find their meaning only side by side with others' (Agamben 1999: 30). Agamben compares this microcosm, the significance of which is dependent upon its 'living and immediate unity with the great world of divine creation' (Agamben 1999: 31), with the apparently similar but actually quite different institution of the modern gallery. The latter is precisely shut off from the rest of the world about which it is not necessarily supposed to tell us anything. According to Agamben, in stark contrast to the view of art implied by the 'cabinet of wonder', 'art has now built its own world for itself' (Agamben 1999: 33). It has become autonomous: it is a law unto itself.

While Adorno might have been wary of the polemical attempt to overcome the autonomy of art and directly to re-establish its cognitive significance that Agamben goes on to develop, he shares a great deal of Agamben's reading of what has been involved in art's becoming autonomous. A good way of exploring Adorno's view of what is won and lost when art becomes autonomous – and also a good way of beginning to get to grips with some of his most important forebears in the history of philosophical aesthetics – is to examine briefly his reception of Kant's and Hegel's aesthetics.

In discussing the way in which the culture industry has made the idea of taste outmoded in the previous chapter, I touched on Kant's insistence that aesthetic judgement must be autonomous. For Kant, aesthetic judgement must not be based on an interest in the existence of an object, nor can it yield any knowledge of the object it judges. We need to focus here on the second of these prescriptions. I can have all sorts of knowledge about, for example, a painting I like, such as Turner's *Steamer in a Snowstorm* (1842). I can know its physical shape and size, what materials were used to make it, the circumstances of its composition, even its place and significance in the history of the development of Western visual art. For Kant, interesting as all of this might be, it is quite distinct from aesthetic judgement. There is no necessary connection between what we might know about a painting and whether it pleases me; just because a painting has certain definable features does not mean that I will like it. This does not entail, as it may seem, that Kant thinks aesthetic judgement is merely subjective; on the contrary, he thinks that the judgement 'this is beautiful' contains the legitimate demand that others agree with me. I cannot, however, compel anyone to agree with me because proof for such a judgement is unavailable to me.

This is only a very brief account of Kant's *Critique of the Power of Judgement*, with the whole of which Adorno engaged on a number of different occasions. What is fundamentally to be emphasized is that Kant focused in his aesthetics, in accord with the procedure of his philosophy as a whole, not on the *object* judged but on the *subjective* process of judgement itself. He insisted in particular that aesthetic judgement is not to be determined by pre-established cognitive or moral categories. This entails that it can yield neither cognition nor moral insight. Art's autonomy is won as its cognitive and moral status is lost, or, at least, seriously compromised. As much as he was indebted to Kant's view of aesthetic judgement, Adorno was also profoundly influenced by Hegel's critique of Kant's aesthetics in his *Aesthetics: Lectures on Fine Art* (delivered, 1823, 1826 and 1828–9; first published posthumously, 1835). Hegel did not want to slip back behind Kant's establishment of the autonomy of art in which the significance of art would be directly deducible from pre-established moral or cognitive categories. However, he does not think that Kant's aesthetics goes far enough in its attempt to steer between a view that would reduce aesthetic judgements to mere opinions and a view that would insist that any aesthetic judgement could be directly justified in ordinary philosophical terms. Although Hegel acknowledges that Kant's account is not subjectivistic in the sense of having to do with mere opinion, he does think that Kant has too little to say about art objects as such, and that, in the end, his account of the creation and judgement of art refers only to the subject, in however qualified a fashion. Kant claims that aesthetic judgement is binding but not because it has to do with anything like the truth of the objects that it judges. This is a major omission in Kant's aesthetics, according to Hegel, caused by the fact that his aesthetics is ultimately based on an account of feeling, 'the indefinite dull region of the spirit' (Hegel 1975a: 32). The problem with investigation into feeling is that it is all too happy to remain with what is merely subjective, 'instead of immersing itself in the thing at issue i.e. in the work of art, plumbing its depths, and in addition relinquishing mere subjectivity and its states' (Hegel 1975a: 31). Although Hegel inherits Kant's refusal of the attempt to establish rules for the production of art, he insists that nonetheless philosophy of art 'has to determine what the beautiful is as such' (Hegel 1975a: 18).

These ideas, first of all about the development of art and also about what is gained and lost in its becoming autonomous, provide the crucial context for *Aesthetic Theory*. It is not simply the case, for Adorno, that the understanding of art has changed over time and that we now have a more or less settled definition with which to work. Rather, the way in which art has developed must be understood as part of its definition:

> [M]uch that was not art – cultic works, for instance – has over the course of history metamorphosed into art; and much that was once art is that no longer. Posed from on high, the question whether something such as film is or is no longer art leads nowhere. Because art is what it has become, its concept refers to what it does not contain . . . Art can be understood only by its laws of movement, not according to any set of invariants. It is defined by its relation to what it is not. The specifically artistic in art must be derived concretely from its other; that alone would fulfil the demands of a materialistic-dialectical aesthetics.
>
> (AT: 3)

Most significant for the argument I am developing in this chapter – and indeed for this book's concern with Adorno's understanding of 'dialectic', which is clearly invoked at the end of this passage – is the insistence that art 'is defined by its relation to what it is not'. Again, this kind of definition contains Adorno's suspicion of definitions. There is an irony in claiming that something is defined by its relation to its opposite because a definition is meant to provide a clear and *positive* statement of what something is or of what it means. Definition is disambiguation; that is, a definition is supposed to give us as precise as possible an account of what something is so that we don't mistake it for something else that it is not. However, a definition of art that would simply leave aside *what art is not* would fail to grasp *what art is* because art, for Adorno, can be understood only once its separation from reality – that is, from what art is not – is included when we think of 'art'. A definition that defines its object in terms of what its object is not, moreover, cannot be established once and for all. This is the case because art's relation to its opposite is not fixed. The relation between art and reality is a process. Adorno wants to write a 'dialectical aesthetics' in the sense that art cannot be conceived without relation to its opposite and in the sense that that relation is a result of development. It is a '*materialistic*-dialectical aesthetics' because aesthetics stems from consideration of actual particulars – that is, from both actual artworks and actual reality – rather than merely conceptual categories emptied of any content. Art can be understood only through its changing negative relation to society.

SOCIAL ANTITHESIS OF SOCIETY

Now that I have given a sketch of Adorno's approach to the 'definition' of 'art', we need to consider in greater depth how this approach operates in Adorno's aesthetics. Near the beginning of *Aesthetic Theory*, Adorno states that 'Art is the social antithesis of society, not immediately deducible from it' (AT: 8 [translation modified]). For Adorno, an important way into thinking about art's relation to society, and thus about what art is, is to ask whether art is a thing. These questions – 'What is art's relation to society?' and 'Is art a thing?' – are connected, according to Adorno, because all currently existing things themselves have to be understood in the way that they are part of society; that is, in the way that they are socially mediated. These questions are dealt with in an intricate but revealing passage from *Aesthetic Theory*:

> Art that is simply a thing is an oxymoron. Yet the development of this oxymoron is nevertheless the inner direction of contemporary art. Art is motivated by a conflict: Its enchantment, a vestige of its magical phase, is constantly repudiated as unmediated sensual immediacy by the progressive disenchant-ment of the world, yet without its ever being possible finally to obliterate this magical element. Only in it is art's mimetic character preserved, and its truth is the critique that, by its sheer existence, it levels at a rationality that has

become absolute. Emancipated from its claim to reality, the enchantment is itself part of enlightenment: Its semblance disenchants the disenchanted world. This is the dialectical ether in which art today takes place.

(AT: 58)

I want to focus on what this passage tells us about two features of art on Adorno's account: that modern art especially both is and is not a thing; and that art is in some sense dialectical. The opening two sentences of this passage sum up a view of modern art that Adorno had been attempting to elaborate since his *Philosophy of New Music*. It is important to take seriously Adorno's

MODERNISM AND NEW MUSIC

It is misleading to suggest that Adorno's aesthetics focuses on Modernist art just because that was the art of his time. Adorno thinks that Modernism presents philosophical interpretation with a number of quite specific questions. Modernist works throw into doubt the very existence of art as such because of their break with traditional forms, genres and techniques. While a range of Modernist works, such as the poetry of Charles Baudelaire (1821–67), the drama of the playwright and novelist Samuel Beckett (1906–89), the novels of Franz Kafka (1883–1924) and James Joyce (1882–1941), and the painting of Pablo Picasso (1881–1973), are important to Adorno's aesthetics, his most sustained engagement is with the 'new music' of the Second Viennese School of composers, primarily Arnold Schoenberg (1874–1951), Alban Berg (1885–1935, by whom Adorno was taught composition in Vienna) and Anton Webern (1883–1945). Led by Schoenberg, these composers broke with the established way of composing music. Rather than composing in a particular key, in which specific notes are included and others excluded as dissonant, the Second Viennese School composed pieces in which any musical note could be used. This method of composition is usually known as 'atonal', although Schoenberg resisted the application of this term to his own music. In *Philosophy of New Music*, Adorno compares Schoenberg's response to the situation in which music found itself at the beginning of the twentieth century with that of the Russian composer Igor Stravinsky (1882–1971), who, in contrast to Schoenberg, attempted directly to re-establish traditional methods of composition.

claim that the oxymoron according to which art both is and is not 'that-thing-there' is central to contemporary art in particular. This is the case with Modernist art in particular because, on the one hand, it refuses recourse to any pre-established definition of art and is thus simply a thing, while, on the other hand, it has also radically severed itself from any social function and therefore does not partake of the general continuum of ordinary things. It is to this problem that Adorno's aesthetics – and his *Aesthetic Theory* in particular – responds.

By virtue of not being directly reducible to a part of reality, art is opposed to it. But art is 'the *social* antithesis of society'. As in Adorno's connected argument that art both is and is not a thing, this claim initially seems paradoxical because art would appear to be opposed, in some sense, to what it is in itself. Again, the significance of what it might mean for art to be the 'social antithesis of society' is brought into focus by Adorno's consideration of the way in which art is or is not a thing. Crucially, 'artworks are only able to become other than thing by becoming a thing' (AT: 86). Artworks can only criticize existing reality by making themselves real because otherwise, simply, they would never exist in the first place. Thus, art's critical aspect relies on its being like what it criticizes. This argument, however, works both ways: art is social by virtue of the fact that it is critical of society (AT: 225). For Adorno, it is autonomous art that has this socially critical function precisely because, as we have seen, autonomous art is emancipated from having to perform any specific, pre-established social role. Simply by existing as something unique, by obeying its own law, autonomous art stands in contradiction to a society in which everything must be exchangeable for everything else. This asocial – or even antisocial – nature of art is its negation of existing society.

AGAINST COMMITMENT

Adorno, therefore, views art as inherently critical of society. However, his aesthetics resists the idea of 'political art' without relinquishing art's relation to politics or to society. Adorno views contemporary art that explicitly sets out to fulfil some sort of socio-critical role as betraying art's polemical stance towards society. This is made most clear in a number of important essays from Adorno's collection of literary criticism, *Notes to Literature*. It is significant that these essays are found in a collection which would look from one point of view to be suspiciously bourgeois. Lengthy discussions of the work of sometimes politically conservative writers are interspersed with often fragmentary reflections on what appear to be mere personal prefer-ences, along with repeated rebukes to authors whose political engagement has come to define their work. Adorno sets out his rejection of political art in his essay 'Commitment'. In the opening pages of this essay he responds both to a number of plays by the French philosopher and writer Jean-Paul Sartre (1905–80) and to his manifesto for a committed literature, *What is Literature?* (1948). Sartre wants to answer the questions 'Why does one write?' and 'For whom does one write?' (Sartre 2001: xxiii). Literature is to have a clearly defined purpose, for Sartre, according to which the free author directly appeals to free readers to act (Sartre 2001: 122). This view of literature motivates Sartre's barely qualified preference for prose over poetry; where the latter is concerned with the fabric and quality of words in themselves, in the former words are utilized to some end. 'Prose is, in essence, utilitarian. I would readily define the prose-writer as a man who *makes use* of words' (Sartre 2001: 11).

Adorno adduces a number of objections to the position represented by Sartre. The latter's privileging of literature on the grounds that it aims at meaning, in his particular sense of *an appeal* from author to reader, is suspect because it ignores the fact that meaning, as it were, inside a work of literature is different from meaning outside a work of literature (NL II: 77). While it never detaches itself entirely from what it means in ordinary speech, no word in a play, poem or even the most realistic novel means exactly what it would mean outside that work. Adorno purposely gives the simplest instance of this: the word 'was'. I have just taken a book down from the shelf (it is Aldous Huxley's *Crome Yellow*, as it happens). If I open it more or less at random, I read: 'But Denis was terribly distressed, and his emotion was intensified when, looking up at her face, he saw that the trace of tears, involuntary tears of pain, lingered on her eyelashes' (Huxley 2004: 89). While this book, like each of Huxley's early novels, might indeed be a satire on the cultural scene of the 1920s, and might, therefore, be more or less loosely based on a host of real people and events, whatever goes into it is transformed by the fact that the novel separates itself from merely factual description of that scene and of those people and events. Denis did not exist; he was *not* terribly distressed. Of course, this simple point has a great many complex consequences, from the question of precisely what the appearance of reality in works of literature entails, to the question, upon which Adorno briefly touches in his lectures on *Problems of Moral Philosophy*, whether it is allowable to think of literature as illustrating ethical problems in various ways (PMP: 158). The central contention remains that Sartre's insistence on meaning as the foundation, so to speak, of literature is open to question on the basis of the simplest literary experience.

Perhaps even more damagingly to Sartre, Adorno aligns his position with the conservative demand that art should give you something, that you should be able to get something out of it. On this kind of view, art must return your investment. Sartre's outlook is therefore conservative both because it requires that art satisfy the demand that it give you something and because it assumes that meaning is straightforwardly available. For Adorno, on the contrary, art refuses this demand that something can always be extracted from anything:

> Those who sing the praises of binding ties will be more likely to find Sartre's *No Exit* profound than to listen patiently to a text in which language rattles the cage of meaning and through its distance from meaning rebels from the outset against a positive assumption of meaning.

> (NL II: 78)

Art opposes what is real not through the declaration of explicit political opinions but through its existence as art; that is, as something that both is real and is radically opposed to reality.

Adorno further elaborates on the way that we might understand the social significance of specific works of art in the opening sentences of his 'On Lyric Poetry and Society', which was originally delivered as a talk on German radio. As was often his way when introducing his lectures, he opens with a warning against misconstruing his title. What is to be feared is that the title 'On Lyric Poetry and Society' does not suggest attention to lyric poems but the filing away of them under sociological categories. The poems would thus become examples of an established sociological thesis (NL I: 37–8). Adorno wishes, however, 'to reveal something essential about the basis of [the poems'] quality'; that is, he attempts to penetrate the works as deeply as possible in order to grasp their social nature. An approach to the relation between lyric poems and society that simply deals in established sociological categories remains exterior to the poems themselves. The lyric poem – usually viewed as the vehicle of the most highly subjective emotional states – is thus precisely social and universal according to the view of art's relation to society that we have already encountered in Adorno's aesthetics. That is, the universality of the lyric poem

> is not the universality of simply communicating what others are unable to communicate. Rather, immersion in what has taken individual form elevates the

lyric poem to the status of something universal by making manifest something
not distorted, not grasped, not yet subsumed.

(NL I: 38)

Again, therefore, the universality of any particular work is established by
way of its uniqueness. Moreover, Adorno goes on to say that the solitude so
often insisted upon as essential to lyric poetry is social in the sense that it is
imposed by an individualistic society (NL I: 38). What is crucial, as Adorno's
opening remarks sought to make clear, is that this relation is not established
by anything that lyric poetry declares, but rather by what, as it were, it is.
We need to turn now to the significance of this insistence for Adorno's view
of the criticism of works of art.

AESTHETICS AND CRITICISM

We need to reflect on the image from 'On Lyric Poetry and Society' of
reaching into the artwork in order to grasp its social or philosophical
significance. On the one hand, the 'truth-content' of any work of art is to be
found in it, not in the philosophical or social categories that can be applied
to it from outside. Adorno is keen to make a similar point in the 'Draft
Introduction' to *Aesthetic Theory*. 'Applied philosophy,' he remarks, 'a priori
fatal, reads out of works that it has invested with an *air* of concretion nothing
but its own theses' (AT: 352). It is not just that the kind of philosophical
reading condemned here is tendentious – that is, it is programmed only ever
to find what it is looking for – but, moreover, the problem is that it reads
theses out of artworks at all. The 'truth-content' of artworks, for Adorno,
does not reside in any thesis into which they might somehow be translated.
As soon as artworks are rendered into conceptual summaries, their real
significance has been lost. On the other hand, as Lambert Zuidervaart (1991:
194–7) has shown in his insightful commentary on *Aesthetic Theory*, the 'truth-
content' of an artwork cannot simply be pointed to in them, as if it were
readily accessible in them without the labour of philosophical interpretation.

We can begin to get a better sense of the background to Adorno's view
that artworks demand philosophical interpretation if we briefly look at
Hegel's version of this thesis, and, perhaps more prominently still for
Adorno, at the account of how artworks require philosophical interpretation
in the work of his friend, the philosopher and critic Walter Benjamin
(1892–1940). First, Adorno agrees with Hegel's contention that while art
is not to be viewed simply as a vehicle for instruction, nor can it be viewed

simply as a source of mere enjoyment and that, therefore, 'What is now aroused in us by works of art is not just immediate enjoyment but our judgement also' (Hegel 1975a: 11). It is in this sense, then, that 'Art awaits its own explanation' (AT: 353). In his essay 'The Concept of Criticism in German Romanticism', Benjamin gives a detailed account of how artworks themselves demand their completion by interpretation. He argues that in Romantic philosophy of art – chiefly that of Novalis (pseudonym of Friedrich von Hardenberg, 1772–1801) and of the brothers Friedrich and August von Schlegel (1772–1829 and 1767–1845, respectively) – criticism is not comprised of mere judgements of taste but rather it 'comprises the knowledge of its object' (Benjamin 1996a: 143). Benjamin's dissertation is essentially an elaboration of this claim. For the Romantics on Benjamin's reading, criticism of artworks 'is far less the judgment of a work than the method of its consummation' (Benjamin 1996a: 153). What this means is that criticism does not necessarily have the sense of an evaluative judgement, but it is rather the coming to fruition of the knowledge already inherent in the artwork itself. 'Insofar as criticism is knowledge of the work of art, it is its self-knowledge; insofar as it judges the artwork, this occurs in the latter's self-judgment' (Benjamin 1996a: 151). This emphasis on criticism as the consummation of something already latent but unrealized in artworks illuminates Adorno's insistence, on the one hand, that artworks should not be interpreted by means of applied philosophy, and his claim, on the other hand, that art requires its fulfilment through philosophy. According to Adorno, 'what the work demands from its beholder is knowledge, and indeed, knowledge that does justice to it: The work wants its truth and untruth to be grasped' (AT: 15). The demand for the truth of artworks is made by the works themselves, not one that the beholder issues regardless of what the works require.

However, although they do indeed demand philosophical interpretation, artworks cannot fully be translated into conceptual terms: 'Artworks that unfold to contemplation and thought without any remainder are not artworks' (AT: 121). Artworks are explicable, but not entirely. A decisive influence on Adorno's nuanced understanding of how artworks both demand philosophical interpretation and are resistant to it is a remarkable book which he read in his youth, *The Spirit of Utopia*, by the German Marxist thinker Ernst Bloch (1885–1977). Indeed, Adorno remarked late on in his career that he had never written anything that did not refer in some way to Bloch's book (NL II: 212). *The Spirit of Utopia* is frequently described as an 'imaginative' work; its combination of biblical commentary, philosophy of music, Western and Eastern mysticism and heterodox Marxism is certainly that. However, there is a danger that this way of describing this book will detract from its very significant philosophical importance for Adorno. One of its main aims is to emphasize that art's significance is missed when it is seen as a matter only of personal preference. Bloch (2000: 3) suggests instead that art is a question of 'the true, the real'. Music in particular, for Bloch, is a kind of understanding, but it is nevertheless distinct from ordinary philosophical knowledge because 'the ear hears more than the concept can explain' (Bloch 2000: 139). It is important, therefore, to emphasize two aspects of Bloch's view of art in general and of music in particular. First, art cannot be directly conceptualized; that is, it cannot be turned immediately into philosophy as philosophy is already established. Second, this is not because art is simply irrelevant to philosophy but, much more significantly, that it has access to a kind of knowledge that philosophy does not have prior to its confrontation with artistic experience. Bloch (2000: 14 [my emphasis]) claims that 'the deeply moved listener immediately *knows and comprehends*' more than can be laid out in ordinary philosophical terms. It is philosophy's task not to impose its established schemes on artistic experience but rather to attend to and to draw out the knowledge and comprehension already implicit in experience of art.

For Adorno, this element of the resistance of artworks to philosophical interpretation is especially true of Modernist art. If it is true, as Hegel declared at the beginning of the nineteenth century, that 'The philosophy of art is therefore a greater need in our day than it was in days when art by itself as art yielded full satisfaction' (Hegel 1975: 11), then, for Adorno, this situation is both especially acute and radically altered with regard to Modernist works. On the one hand, the challenge to traditional notions of the value of harmony posed by Schoenberg's music, or to ideas about poetic decorum by Baudelaire's poetry, means that such artworks demand renewed reflection on the very nature of art. On the other hand, the very force with which traditional artistic categories are indeed challenged by Modernist works entails that they cannot, in fact, yield entirely to understanding. 'The task of aesthetics', Adorno declares, 'is not to comprehend artworks as hermeneutical objects; in the contemporary situation, it is their incomprehensibility that needs to be comprehended' (AT: 118).

These important aspects of Adorno's view of the relationship between art and philosophy are central to his attempt to comprehend the incomprehensible in his essay 'Trying to Understand *Endgame*', on a play by the Irish novelist and dramatist Samuel Beckett. In Beckett's play, Hamm

– the domineering but wheelchair-bound and blind main character – and Clov – his grudging carer, incapable of sitting down and with a range of undefined 'things to do' – share with two dustbins a sort of purgatorial living-room in which no real living takes place. In the dustbins reside Nagg, Hamm's 'Accursed progenitor' (Beckett 1990: 96), and Nell, Nagg's female counter-part. Clov occasionally looks out of the two windows on either side of the back of the stage at what we might only assume is some sort of post-catastrophic landscape. He wheels Hamm around the room and rather touchingly presents him with the half-finished model of a dog, on which, as if in a kind of second-year woodwork class, he is working diligently. More disconcertingly, Clov discovers he has a flea in his shirt and that there is a rat in the kitchen, both of which must be exterminated, not so much because of the irritation and threat to good hygiene that they pose, but in case they should hold out the possibility of the renewed evolution of the human race from the humble genetic beginnings that they represent. Clov consistently threatens to leave Hamm, although, despite going so far as to dress for a journey, he never does. For his part, Hamm issues various commands, berates, occasionally bargains with, and otherwise abuses Nagg, and requests a painkiller from Clov with increasing frustration. (They have run out of painkillers.) The curtain falls on the tableau of Clov staring at the recumbent Hamm with which the play began.

While what I have just provided might look like a brief description of the characters of *Endgame*, along with a summary of its main action, it is far from clear that that is what I have achieved. This is not necessarily because I am not very good at such things. Rather, Hamm and Clov are not really characters. Their distorted and damaged forms, missing this or that faculty, point to their incapacity as the kind of human beings that could be 'characters' at all. Moreover, the play itself – the very first line of which, spoken by Clov, is 'Finished, it's finished, nearly finished, it must be nearly finished' (Beckett 1990: 93) – cannot really be described as having any action. (The reviewer and Beckett scholar Vivian Mercier once famously said, in reference to the two acts of another of Beckett's plays, *Waiting for Godot*, 'Nothing happens, twice.') This radicalization of aesthetic form is, for Adorno, the most important characteristic of Beckett's work and the basis of its opposition to that of a playwright and theorist like Sartre. Whereas Sartre's plays merely serve to illustrate a set of ideas which are already decided upon, in Beckett literary form 'overtakes what is expressed and changes it' (NL I: 241). Moreover, Sartre still assumes that the modes of the expression of meaning open to traditional works of art are equally open to modern works that must, however, respond to the world bereft of clearly definable, secure meaning in the wake of the Second World War and the Nazi genocide. Sartre thinks that dramatic meaning – that is, the established criteria of dramatic form – can straightforwardly contain ideas about the meaninglessness of reality. He neither fully grasps the real meaninglessness of contemporary reality nor does he achieve aesthetic meaning because his plays fail to respond adequately to the contemporary situation. Adorno's wariness of philosophy's pretensions to a wholly adequate understanding of reality is a major topic of the following chapter; his view of the characteristic features of contemporary reality will be set out more fully later.

SUMMARY

While art does hold an especially privileged place in Adorno's thought, it is not simply and absolutely serious for him. That is, art is both removed from the web of deadening seriousness that the world has become and, in being removed in this way, it seriously presents the possibility that the world might be otherwise. Adorno holds that art has an important relation to society, and that it demands philosophical interpretation, but that in most versions of political and philosophical readings of artworks their specifically aesthetic status is missed. The question of art's nature and status is especially acutely posed, for Adorno, by Modernist works, such as Beckett's plays and the music of Arnold Schoenberg.

4

THINGS, THOUGHT
AND BEING RIGHT

TRUTH AND FORM

We saw in the last chapter that Adorno is suspicious of attempts decisively to separate aesthetics from epistemology (the theory of knowledge, of what and how we know), from metaphysics (the theory of the basic features of reality) and from moral theory (the theory of what we ought (and ought not) to do). This suspicion is aimed not only at bolstering the claims of art and the aesthetic but at indicating the centrality of the aesthetic to epistemology, metaphysics and morals. There are significant general similarities between Adorno's conceptions of thought and of art. For him, art points beyond existence while at the same time it nevertheless exists. The same kind of relation to existence and what does not yet exist obtains in the case of thought. According to the 'Introduction' to *Negative Dialectics*, thought 'serves' the non-existent, which is to say that thought is 'a piece of existence that reaches, however negatively, to the non-existent' (ND: 57 [translation modified]). The idea that thought, like art, is in the service of an existence opposed to the current wrong state of the world is strikingly anticipated earlier in the 'Introduction' when Adorno states that 'Dialectics serves reconciliation' (ND: 6 [translation modified]). Thought serves non-existence in that it serves a world different from the current one. The end or purpose of thought is not immediately identifiable with specific utilitarian purposes; rather, thought points to an existence in which such purposes cease to dominate.

There are, then, important general analogies in Adorno's work between the structures of art and of thought, having to do in particular with the relations between art and thought and existence and non-existence. A more specific relation between thought and the aesthetic can be found in Adorno's view that the aesthetic form of truth – that is, truth's expression in the writing of philosophical of texts – is fundamental to truth itself. The composition of philosophy is essential to philosophy's truth-content itself, rather than a secondary concern with the way in which established dogmas might be communicated. Just as music must be composed in order to be music at all, so must philosophy:

> [I]nstead of reducing philosophy to categories, one would in a sense have to compose it first. Its course must be a ceaseless self-renewal, by its own strength as well as in friction with whatever standard it may have. The crux is what happens in it, not a thesis or a position – the texture, not the deductive or inductive course of one-track minds.
>
> (ND: 33)

I remarked in 'Why Adorno?' that Adorno resists the idea that philosophy can adequately be summarized. He opposes the view, which he contends is prevalent in the kind of philosophy established as the academic standard, that the truth or untruth of philosophy is reducible to a series of claims or assertions. Instead, integral to philosophy's truth or untruth is the expression of those claims or assertions, the way in which they are developed throughout a philosophical text and authorship, and the order in which they come. When the content of a philosophical authorship is reduced to a set of bullet-points to be regurgitated preferably under exam conditions, then the truth of that philosophy has been missed. This view means Adorno disobeys many of the rules of professional academic practice. Sloppily essayistic, it might therefore be alleged, his work belongs on the coffee-table but has somehow ended up on the university library shelf.

However, Adorno's works are not just Saturday reviews posing as philosophy. We can get a fuller sense of his refusal of the stark opposition between truth and expression – and the dismissal of the latter that goes with this opposition – if we look at his comments on the form of the aphorism and, first, of the essay. In his 'The Essay as Form', Adorno states most of the central features of his view of what thought is, placing special emphasis on the way that the restricted space and particular focus of the essay suggest a departure from the traditional view of truth and intellectual rigour (see Jarvis

1998: 138). Adorno jettisons the disregard for the form in which objects are presented not out of some romantically conceived notion that philosophical work must be expressive. Rather, disregard for form short-circuits the objective presentation at which supposedly rigorous philosophy aims: 'In its allergy to forms as mere accidental attributes, the spirit of science and scholarship comes to resemble that of rigid dogmatism' (NL I: 5). The forms of scientifically conceived philosophy are merely conventional and do not change with the objects being discussed. Towards the end of 'The Essay as Form', Adorno demonstrates his contention that the form of philosophy is part of its meaning by pointing to one of his favourite concerns in the interpretation of the philosophical tradition: the contradiction inherent in Kant's thinking. The goal of philosophy for Kant, according to Adorno, is the establishment of a genuine humanity freed from inhumanity; that is, the establishment of Utopia. This insight, however, is hindered by 'the form of his thought, epistemology', which reduces the conditions of the possibility of any real thing to what has already existed (NL I: 21). When the form of philosophy is disregarded, evaluation of the truth of its content is impossible.

The reflection on the form of *Minima Moralia* in its 'Dedication' is likewise fundamental to an understanding of the role of philosophical composition in Adorno's thinking. *Minima Moralia* is made up of 153 aphorisms, or short reflections on various topics. Even if, like the essay only more so, the aphorism is a short statement that addresses a particular concern without

APHORISMS

An aphorism is a short, pithy statement, often treating a specific thing or topic but aiming to express a general truth. There is an important tradition of philosophical aphorisms which includes, for example, the aphorisms of the Duc de la Rochefoucauld (1613–80) and the 'maxims and arrows' of Nietzsche. Aphoristic expression allows for particular features of individual experience to come to the fore and to escape the strictures of oppressively universal categories, while not relinquishing the claim of such experience to greater significance than might initially be apparent. As J.M. Bernstein has recently commented: 'The aphoristic procedure of *Minima Moralia* can . . . usefully be seen as a corrective to theoretical colonisation; it aims to express as well as reflect (on) the experience of the individual' (Bernstein 2001: 45 n. 7).

always going back to first principles, it is not simply that there are as many different thoughts in *Minima Moralia* as there are aphorisms. This is not the case, of course, because many of the individual aphorisms follow on from and anticipate others and also because a number of central topics are frequently developed over a number of connected aphorisms. It is also not the case for the more compelling reason that *Minima Moralia* has been 'schooled' by Hegel, which is to say that it cannot simply abandon the claim to totality of Hegel's system. The aphorism is a central bone of contention in Adorno's revision of Hegel's dialectic: 'Dialectical theory, abhorring anything isolated, cannot admit aphorisms as such.' (MM: 16). Hegel, however, too readily dismissed the particular in his concern to attain a universally binding philosophical system. This was, according to Adorno, a betrayal of Hegel's own insistence that philosophy should immerse itself in the particular rather than overstepping it on the way to the universal. In such a betrayal, both particular and universal are missed because the universal resides in the particular. This is especially so for the kind of theory of individualistic society at which *Minima Moralia* aims and, therefore, 'social analysis can learn incomparably more from individual experience than Hegel conceded' (MM: 17). The aphoristic form of *Minima Moralia* is dictated by the scrupulous attention to individual experience, which, in turn, will yield greater insight into society than mere adherence to the norms of sociological science.

PARTICULAR AND UNIVERSAL

This consideration of the importance of aphorisms to the theoretical aims of *Minima Moralia* clearly opens up a number of further questions central to Adorno's conception of philosophy. Most significant, perhaps, have to do with his idea of dialectic and, in turn, with his relation to Hegel, both of which I will address in this section and the following one.

Sweeping generalizations with regard to Adorno's intellectual commitments are usually best avoided, but one that most commentators on his work allow themselves is that his debt to Hegel is very great indeed. This debt is not, however, straightforward. Indeed, perhaps one of Adorno's best-known declarations – 'The whole is the false', from *Minima Moralia* – is a direct inversion of Hegel's statement that 'the True is the whole' from the *Phenomenology of Spirit* (Hegel 1977: 11). As is frequently emphasized in discussion of Adorno's written style, what look like direct statements need to be set in context in order fully to be understood. In fact, Adorno offers a more nuanced reading of Hegel's claim that 'the True is the whole' in an essay on the conservative cultural criticism of the early twentieth-century German writer Oswald Spengler (1880–1936) included in *Prisms*:

> The superstitious belief that the greatness of philosophy lies in its grandiose aspects is a bad heritage of Idealism – as though the quality of a painting depends on the sublimity of its subject-matter. Great themes prove nothing about the greatness of the knowledge. If, as Hegel argues, the whole is what is true, then it is so only if the force of the whole is absorbed into the knowledge of the particular.
>
> (P: 62 [translation modified])

Adorno makes the point that is echoed in a number of places throughout his work: just because a philosophy deals with big issues, it does not follow that it is great; just because a painting is of something sublime, it does not follow that it is sublime. One of the features of the way in which Adorno reads is that he is as likely to find genuine insight in works that deal with topics that have been classified as minor by mainstream tradition or whose procedure condemns them to eccentricity. This is one reason why Hegel's claim that 'the True is the whole' cannot merely rely – to the detriment of the particular – on the supposedly greater force of the whole. Indeed, for Adorno, Hegel already had something of this sense of the relation between part and whole:

> There is a sort of suspended quality associated with his philosophy, in accordance with the idea that truth cannot be grasped in any individual thesis or any delimited position . . . Nothing can be understood in isolation, everything is to be understood only in the context of the whole, with the awkward qualification that the whole in turn lives only in the individual moments.
>
> (HTS: 91)

This would not be a bad description of Adorno's own writing. The universal must penetrate the knowledge of the particular rather than merely contain it, if the universal is to have any force at all. This insistence is at the root of Adorno's claim that individual experience is as central – indeed, more central – to social theory as are broader social trends. This relation between individual and general, as Adorno's remark on Hegel from his essay on Spengler makes clear, works the other way too. The universal enables understanding of the particular as universal, rather than merely providing the framework into which the latter is slotted in order to be forgotten.

All of this might make it seem that Adorno modifies Hegel's dialectic in order to facilitate a kind of negotiation between the terms of the various oppositions that Hegel had prematurely closed down in favour of one term or the other. Dialectic, it might appear, is moderation. However, Adorno vigorously rejected any appeal to a golden mean. Dialectic does not establish itself in the comfortable middle ground between opposing terms, content with 'the serene demonstration of the fact that there are two sides to everything' (MM: 247). As Adorno put it earlier in *Minima Moralia*, 'the dialectic advances by way of extremes' (MM: 86). Dialectics is not a kind of intellectual relaxation. It does not simply point to the contradictions discernible in everything and thus excuse itself from engaging with anything. Adorno entitles one of the most important aphorisms to consider dialectic in *Minima Moralia* 'Bequest' because it attempts to set out the main tasks that Benjamin's writings have set contemporary thought. The idea of a 'bequest' in this aphorism also touches on the way that dialectic responds to non-dialectical thought: 'Dialectical thought is an attempt to break through the coercion of logic by its own means' (MM: 150). It thus takes seriously what is bequeathed it in the gaps and contradictions of the philosophical heritage. There is no way to defeat the compulsory character of logic other than to turn the force of that compulsion against itself.

KNOWLEDGE AS POSSESSION

Adorno's elaboration of dialectical thought, then, includes a consideration of how it relates to the forms of traditional philosophical logic. In addition, the idea of dialectic itself hardly originated with Adorno and so his attempt to develop a dialectical mode of thinking needs to examine and evaluate previous versions of dialectic itself. According to Adorno, the main problem with earlier thinking that has proclaimed itself dialectical is that it was not sufficiently dialectical. This is because, as he put it in his initial explanation of the title of his philosophical masterpiece, *Negative Dialectics*, 'dialectics meant to achieve something positive by means of negation' (ND: xix). The task of *Negative Dialectics*, on the contrary, is to preserve the unrelenting focus of dialectical thinking and to intensify it by freeing it of its implicitly affirmative aim. Dialectics as such, therefore, is properly negative. Adorno objects to positive dialectics on the grounds that if dialectics is pressed into the service of some positive aim, then its focus on the material with which it deals is weakened. Dialectics with a positive aim of this kind becomes like any other portable method with which to achieve an end that has been fixed upon in advance.

Dialectics is not a means for securing knowledge as an established possession. The aim to have knowledge securely in one's possession is, according to Adorno, precisely opposed to philosophy's most important concerns. This is a lesson he took from Benjamin, whose influence on Adorno's view of the philosophical interpretation of artworks I briefly discussed in the previous chapter. Benjamin was perhaps the single most important influence on Adorno's work. Indeed, Raymond Geuss's quip that 'Adorno had an odd fixation on Benjamin' is not altogether unfair if it is taken to indicate the abiding involvement of Adorno's thinking with fundamental concerns of Benjamin's work (Geuss 2005: 163 n. 6). Particularly significant for Adorno's view of knowledge and truth was Benjamin's study of German drama in the baroque era, *The Origin of the German Play of Lamentation* (the English translation of which is somewhat misleadingly titled, *The Origin of German Tragic Drama*) (Benjamin 1998). At first sight, this might seem like a rather esoteric book on a very specific area of German literary history: it is a minutely detailed account of German drama around the time of the Protestant Reformation and of its relationship to its historical circumstances. It is also one of the most important works in twentieth-century philosophy and aesthetic theory. In particular, this book, especially its astonishing 'Epistemo-Critical Prologue', is fundamental to the development of Adorno's view that the aim of philosophy is not simply the secure possession of knowledge. In the process of elaborating a highly original and distinctive programme for philosophy, Benjamin distinguishes sharply between truth, on the one hand, and knowledge, on the other. Philosophy ought to be conceived, Benjamin argues, 'as the representation of truth and not as a guide for the acquisition of knowledge' (Benjamin 1998: 28). Truth, for Benjamin, is unconditional, is not open to question, and pre-exists the attempt to grasp it; knowledge, on the contrary, is questionable and formed only in the consciousness to which it belongs: 'Knowledge is possession. Its very object is determined by the fact that it must be taken possession of – even if in a transcendental sense – in the consciousness' (Benjamin 1998: 29).

Adorno develops this sense of a distinction between knowledge and truth in his denunciation of the desire to be right. He sets this out in a reminiscence that is all too easily recognizable:

The very wish to be right, down to its subtlest form of logical reflection, is an expression of that spirit of self-preservation which philosophy is precisely concerned to break down. I knew someone who invited all the celebrities in epistemology, science and the humanities one after the other, discussed his own system with each of them from first to last, and when none of them dared raise any further arguments against its formalism, believed his position totally impregnable.

(MM: 70)

The mixture of deference to the 'celebrities of epistemology, science and the humanities' and passive intellectual aggression in the desire to establish a 'totally impregnable' position shown by the person recollected here points to a concern not with truth but with approval.

Does Adorno not care, then, whether he is right or wrong? At first sight, his critique of the desire to be right appears to be in danger of recoiling into a kind of controversialism that is frankly careless of whether it is justified or not. In the 'Preface' to *Negative Dialectics*, however, Adorno remarks of what is to come in the body of the book that 'The procedure will not be established but justified. To the best of his ability the author means to put his cards on the table – which is by no means the same as playing the game' (ND: xix [translation modified]). The distinctions that Adorno is trying to draw here, especially the distinction between justification and establishment, are extremely significant. As I noted above, Adorno thinks that what happens in philosophical texts is more important than any set of statements that might be extracted from them. The importance of this idea can be seen again here because, were procedure established, it would be fixed and, in not proceeding anywhere, it would not therefore be a procedure at all. A procedure cannot be justified by pinning it down to foundations established at the outset. By emphasizing justification as opposed to establishment, Adorno suggests that the value of the procedure can be discerned only in how that procedure is conducted rather than in the principles that supposedly ground it.

This kind of distinction between justification and establishment is echoed by Adorno's important idea of 'immanent criticism'. Adorno discusses what he means by 'immanent criticism' – that is, a kind of criticism conducted in the terms of what it is criticizing, rather than in terms established before any material is actually approached – at a number of places in his work. He thinks that criticism must be 'immanent' in the sense that it must be internal to whatever it criticizes; that is, it must attend as closely as possible to its object, rather than imposing externally formulated standards upon it.

Crucially, Adorno also argues that while immanent criticism must immerse itself as deeply as possible in what it criticizes, it must also be independent of it. He expresses this claim in his essay 'Cultural Criticism and

Society', from *Prisms*, in which he argues that 'without consciousness transcending the immanence of culture, immanent criticism itself would be inconceivable: the spontaneous movement of the object can be followed only by someone who is not entirely engulfed by it' (P: 29). While it is imperative to criticize objects in their own terms rather than in pre-established categories applied to them from outside, immanent criticism is only ever possible on the basis of a certain freedom with regard to the object being criticized. Otherwise, the critic ceases to be able to judge anything and is merely carried along by whatever he or she is supposed to criticize. What this position entails is that the strict division between immanence – remaining internal to something – and transcendence – a position separate from and above something – is disavowed. Adorno gives a good idea of what immanent criticism would involve in his claims that we often need to grasp the intention of a philosophical authorship in contradiction with its explicit formulations. Adorno makes this similar point in connection with his discussion of 'how to read Hegel' from his *Hegel: Three Studies*. According to Adorno, 'immanent fidelity to Hegel's intention requires one to supplement or go beyond the text in order to understand it' (HTS: 131). This does not simply mean that, in order to understand a text, we need to have recourse to biographical detail, to the work's historical context, or to manuscripts and notes pertaining to the finished text. Being able to deal confidently with these sources of information is a valuable skill for a critic, for sure. What Adorno means, though, is that Hegel must not only be read by his own standards but must be judged by them, even where he fails to live up to them.

IMPULSE IN THOUGHT

Adorno's preference for justification over foundation is part of his overall criticism of the accepted criteria of philosophical validity. He develops Nietzsche's attack on the usual criteria for objective knowledge, questioning in particular whether thinking is ever dispassionate. In Aphorism 79 from *Minima Moralia*, Adorno argues that an intellect which seeks wholly to free itself from emotion is not strengthened but weakened thereby. In the course of one of his important attempts to dismantle the entire scaffolding of moral theory from Socrates to Kant, *Beyond Good and Evil* (1886), Nietzsche declared, 'The degree and kind of a man's sexuality reaches up into the topmost summit of his spirit' (Nietzsche 1973: 92). Adorno interprets this maxim as having greater than merely psychological significance but as pointing also to the fact that thinking would be impossible without being 'nourished by impulses' (MM: 122). For Adorno, even the most apparently abstract thought contains feeling – fear, desire, melancholy and so on – regarding what is thought about. Crucially, however, he differs from a dominant trend in post-Nietzschean philosophy according to which the insistence on the impossibility of separating thinking from emotion is taken to entail the nullity of reason as such. Adorno defends his view from the charge that it is simply reducible to this kind of irrationalism by admitting that if knowledge cannot attain objectivity it remains 'under the sway of desire'. This does not mean, for Adorno, that the relation between knowledge and desire is entirely severed. On the contrary, impulse, from whose dictatorship knowledge must escape if it is to become knowledge at all, must nevertheless be 'preserved and surpassed' [*aufgehoben*] in thought (MM: 122).

'TO PRESERVE AND TO SURPASS'

The German term *aufheben* (*aufgehoben* is the past participle) is most often translated as 'to sublate'. This is a helpful translation because it comes close to capturing the different senses contained in the German. *Aufheben* can mean 'to preserve', as well as 'to abolish' or 'to cancel out'. Likewise, 'to sublate' means both 'to cancel' and 'to lift up' or 'to elevate'. The idea of sublation is central to Hegel's philosophy. One of the best examples of how something might be cancelled and, as it were, elevated according to Hegel is perhaps also the most famous, from the important 'Preface' to *Phenomenology of Spirit*:

> The bud disappears in the bursting-forth of the blossom, and one might say that the former is refuted by the latter; similarly, when the fruit appears, the blossom is shown up in its turn as a false manifestation of the plant, and the fruit now emerges as the truth of it instead. These forms are not just distinguished from one another, they also supplant one another as mutually incompatible. Yet at the same time their fluid nature makes them moments of an organic unity in which they do not conflict, but in which each is as necessary as the other; and this mutual necessity alone constitutes the life of the whole.
>
> (Hegel 1977: 2)

Significantly, Hegel is talking here about the way that, contrary to the fixation in 'conventional opinion' on the opposition between different philosophies, the disagreement between philosophical views should be seen as the unfolding of truth, rather than simple antagonism. This is important for Adorno, whose engagement with the kind of philosophical positions that he opposes is never just polemical, but is rather concerned to comprehend and surpass the inadequacies that he perceives in them.

One of the most important impulses with which thinking is inextricably involved, according to Adorno, is hope. This view of the mutual implication of thinking and hope deepens the radical separation of Adorno from usually accepted standards for objective thought, on the one hand, and, on the other, it further distances him from important aspects of Nietzsche's critique not only of traditional rationalism but of religion. Adorno compares Nietzsche's rejection of the Christian argument that faith is true because it facilitates hope with his principle of *amor fati*; that is, of the love of fate. 'We might well ask', Adorno comments, 'whether we have more reason to love what happens to us, to affirm what is because it is, than to believe true what we hope.' Nietzsche's position is the affirmation of what exists simply because it exists. While the Christian argument for faith and Nietzsche's concept of *amor fati*, therefore, seem to be as bad as each other, Adorno in fact argues that hope is fundamental to the very idea of truth because otherwise existence, which is recognized as bad, is presented as true. 'In the end hope, wrested from reality by negating it, is the only form in which truth appears' (MM: 98). Again, it is clear from this kind of argument that Adorno refuses any clear separation between what might be classed as epistemological categories (truth, untruth) and moral ones (good, bad). The idea of truth, for Adorno, is inescapably evaluative.

POSITIVISM, CRITIQUES OF IDEALISM AND NEO-ONTOLOGY

I have been arguing that Adorno's commitment to the evaluative nature of truth implies his opposition to many of the dominant trends in philosophy. For Adorno, any philosophy that merely aims to correspond as exactly as possible to matters of fact is conservative. Equally, he views many of the attempts in twentieth-century philosophy – often from apparently very different philosophical traditions – fully to grasp existence as having failed. Those philosophies that proclaim their concretion and their attention to actual particulars are often as empty as the conceptual systems they seek to overcome. This section deals first with the conservatism Adorno sees as implicit in what he calls 'positivist' philosophy before moving on to discuss some of the ways in which positivism's failings are also discernible in the attempt by the German philosopher and sometime advocate of Nazism Martin Heidegger (1889–1976) to re-engage Western philosophy with consideration of the nature of Being as such.

POSITIVISM

Raymond Geuss has offered a usefully succinct definition of positivism from the point of view associated with Adorno: 'In Frankfurt usage a "positivist" is a person who holds (a) that an empiricist account of natural science is adequate, and (b) that all cognition must have essentially the same cognitive structure as natural science' (Geuss 1981: 2). It is useful to bear this provisional definition in mind when we discuss Adorno's frequent engagements with 'positivism', not least because it covers a multitude of sins. So, 'positivism' is the main characteristic of twentieth-century 'analytic philosophy', in which metaphysics is eliminated along with all other non-verifiable and hence meaningless – on this view – areas of thought. This kind of philosophy is associated with Rudolf Carnap (1891–1970) and the 'Vienna Circle' of logicians and philosophers, and with A.J. Ayer, author of the seminal *Language, Truth, and Logic* (1936), who was a contemporary of Adorno's at Oxford. But perhaps Adorno's most sustained and explicit encounter with 'positivism' is in *The Positivist Dispute in German Sociology*, to which he contributed. In opposition to Adorno, the sociologist and philosopher of science Karl Popper (1902–94) advanced the view that 'The method of the social sciences, like that of the natural sciences, consists in trying out tentative solutions to certain problems' (PDGS, 89) before the solutions are decisively if temporarily separated into accepted sheep and refuted goats.

Adorno criticizes the aim of positivist philosophy and science to establish a secure stock of knowledge. We have already seen how, in his criticism of the wish to be right, Adorno questions the value of 'totally impregnable' knowledge (MM: 70). Such a wish betrays a view of knowledge that sees it as a kind of property. The rights to 'intellectual property' enshrined in patent and copyright law are only the clearest expressions of the view that knowledge is a possession. Moreover, this kind of view is connected, for Adorno, to 'conformism, the respectful reiteration of the factual' (MM: 142), which merely sees knowledge as adaptation to what is currently the case. Intellectual conformism depends on the assumption – perhaps the most prominent advocate of which in the philosophical tradition is Kant (Kant 2000: 123) – that every thought is universally communicable to every subject. Adorno's rejection of the principle of the universal communicability of thought is another way in which he criticizes the accepted standards of intellectual validity. Crucially, there is no necessary connection, for Adorno, between expression appropriate to the object presented and expression that is guaranteed to be understood by all. This is because the latter is compelled to follow pre-established patterns of what is already understood, whereas 'the value of a thought is measured by its distance from the continuity of the familiar' (MM: 80).

Despite – or, indeed, because of – its insistence on correspondence to given facts, positivist philosophy apparently deals only with actual, concrete things. Adorno shows why this is the case in his account of intellectual distance; that is, in his account of the way in which the intellect must not be wholly immersed in what it reflects upon if it is to have any purchase on it. This account is qualified, of course, because Adorno believes that thinking cannot be entirely dispassionate; thinking cannot simply be separated from suffering, hope or similar impulses. Nietzsche, as we have seen, is crucial to this aspect of Adorno's rejection of dispassion as a criterion of thinking. Where Nietzsche had objected to Kant's argument that aesthetic judgement should be disinterested because, Nietzsche claimed, it is impossible to behold the statue of a naked woman disinterestedly, Adorno remarks that it is impossible dispassionately to consider the suffering on a global scale with which thought is confronted today. However, precisely because given facts are the facts of the wrong state of the world, for Adorno, distance from them is essential if thinking is to have a claim to truth. That is, thinking's dogged adherence to the *wrong* state of things does not guarantee thinking's *truth*. Moreover, mere reproduction of reality in thought does not even entail an adequate grasp of reality because no thought ever fully expresses reality (MM: 126). This ultimately imperfect match between thought and thing – their non-identity – is crucial, according to Adorno, to the constitution of thought as such. Non-identity is both the guilt of thought (because thought is distant from what it claims to think about) and its freedom (because thought is not bound inescapably to what merely exists). Positivist philosophy refuses to acknowledge the non-identity of thought and thing, and thus bears the guilt of thought without enjoying its freedom.

This failure properly to attend to concrete things – despite the stated intention to do so – is shared, in Adorno's view, by a number of prominent philosophical attempts to overcome idealism. ('Idealism' here does not mean the pursuit of lofty aims, such as, for example, the eradication of poverty; rather, 'idealism' in its philosophical usage refers to the belief that reality in some ultimate sense is related to the contents of our minds.) This similarity between positivism and versions of anti-idealist thought is striking because there are radical differences between avowedly positivistic philosophy and attempts, however unsuccessful in the end, to overcome idealism. Adorno discusses a number of miscarried attempts to overcome idealism, especially in the work that he wrote either in the early phase of his career or that which is based on studies he conducted during this time. This work includes his first published book, *Kierkegaard: Construction of the Aesthetic*; the book based on his doctoral research into the German philosopher Edmund Husserl (1859–1938), translated into English with the title *Against Epistemology*; and the important essay, yet to be translated into English, 'Theses on the Language of the Philosopher'.

Kierkegaard is a detailed study of the work of the Danish philosopher and theologian Søren Kierkegaard (1813–55). Benjamin, in a review of this book, perceptively commented that 'The author's subsequent writings may some day emerge from it' (quoted in Müller-Doohm 2005: 130). The main concern of Adorno's study of Kierkegaard emerges in the second chapter, 'Constitution of Inwardness'. Here, he discusses Kierkegaard's attempt to overcome what is seen as the idealist neglect of actual reality. Kierkegaard argued that this absence of actual reality in idealism could be overcome by a turn to the concretely real individual subject. Adorno described this Kierkegaardian subject as 'objectless inwardness' (KCA: 27). According to Adorno, this attempt to grasp reality miscarries, however, precisely because Kierkegaard's insistence on subjectivity as the be all and end all of reality is ultimately dogmatic. Central to his philosophical focus on subjectivity is Kierkegaard's scrupulous exclusion of everything that does not belong to 'Free, active subjectivity' (KCA: 27). This means, in Adorno's view, that the subject envisaged by Kierkegaard ends up as 'only an isolated subject, surrounded by a dark otherness' (KCA: 29). Adorno is claiming that in cutting the subject off from everything external to it, Kierkegaard has eliminated from his philosophy everything that he had wanted to preserve. 'In the image of the concrete individual,' Adorno writes, 'subjectivity rescues only the rubble of the existent. Subjectivity, in the form of objectless inwardness, mourns in its painful affects for the world of things as for "meaning"' (KCA: 30). In attempting to make subjectivity the ultimate ground of reality in opposition to idealism's neglect of the real, Kierkegaard ends up with a subject that is ultimately stripped of everything that might have made it meaningful.

In a manner similar to Kierkegaard's philosophy, the philosophy of the figure Adorno took to be his great intellectual antagonist, Heidegger, ends up empty. Adorno's antipathy to Heidegger is partly explained by the divergence between Heidegger's sympathy for National Socialism and Adorno's Marxism. However, there are some important philosophical differences between Adorno and Heidegger as well. We need to look briefly at the central concern of Heidegger's philosophy and at Adorno's assessment of it.

There is a coffee-cup here on my desk. It is blue, it has a handle, and, at the moment, it is about two-thirds full of black coffee. It would not really occur to me to say, as well, that this coffee-cup *is*. In fact, what I've already said would imply this. Being is the coffee-cup's most abstract, general feature, the feature that everything else has as well, and thus saying that the coffee-cup 'is' is the least informative statement that I can make about it. Heidegger contests that this view of Being points to the fact that the question of Being has been forgotten by philosophy (Heidegger 1962). Indeed, this is not just any question, but the fundamental question of philosophy. There is, however, a serious obstacle in the way of a direct answer to this question. Being, for Heidegger, is distinct from any actual thing. Being, that is, always transcends – is above and beyond – any actual being. Thus, consideration of existing entities – such as the blue coffee-cup on my desk – does not give access to the real meaning of Being.

Although this is a drastically foreshortened account of Heidegger's work, it is necessary here to emphasize that Adorno saw in Heidegger's division of Being from beings a failed attempt to grasp reality. In 'The Actuality of Philosophy', which was Adorno's initial lecture as a member of the Philosophy Faculty at Frankfurt University, he questions the idea of Being itself. According to Adorno, Being in Heidegger is 'an empty form-principle' (AP: 120). That is, Heidegger's insistence on the distance between actual entities and Being as such entails that the latter is simply inscrutable and that the former are inadequately grasped in Heidegger's philosophy. For Adorno, this means that, despite the apparently immense differences between their philosophical idioms and procedures, both positivist philosophers and Heidegger partake in the conservative affirmation of whatever simply exists. For both positivism and Heidegger, this affirmation is based on a view of reality that ultimately renders it abstract.

Although Adorno commends the aim to overcome idealism, especially, perhaps, in Kierkegaard and Husserl, the attempt to do so has most frequently misfired and ended up merely assuming a concrete actuality that is, in fact, as empty as what it would supersede. This kind of false concretion is matched by the reconciliation – falsely assumed to have been achieved, or, indeed, assumed never to have been required in the first place – between thought and thing envisaged by identity philosophy. Whereas Adorno views thought and thing as non-identical, identity philosophy assumes that concepts are entirely adequate to the objects that they would enable us to know. The false assumption that reconciliation has already been achieved (or was never required) is called 'ideology'. One of the implicit aims of *Negative Dialectics* is to develop an account of identity philosophy's ideological status. Thus, ideology 'lies in the implicit identity of concept and thing' and 'Identity is the primal form of ideology' (ND: 40, 148). Crucially, however, Adorno is not concerned simply to condemn ideology for being untrue. While ideology is false in stating that the reconciliation of thought and thing is already achieved, it is true in containing the wish that it will be:

> The supposition of identity is indeed the ideological element of pure thought, all the way down to formal logic; but hidden in it is also the truth moment of ideology, the pledge that there should be no contradiction, no antagonism. In the simple identifying judgment, the pragmatist, nature-controlling element already joins with a utopian element. 'A' is to be what it is not yet.
>
> (ND: 149–50)

We can hear in ideology what Bloch in *The Spirit in Utopia* described as 'cognition's prayer: May it truly be thus!' (Bloch 2000: 172). Ideology's hope is masked, not annulled, by its assertion that reconciliation has already come about.

DIALECTIC IN THOUGHT AND IN THINGS

Adorno's emphasis on the non-identity of thought and thing is not simply intended as an uncomplicated rejection of identity philosophy. On the contrary, Adorno seeks to show both that identity philosophy cannot overcome this non-identity by simple adherence to given facts and that in it we can discern the wish that thing and thought be reconciled. What reconciliation would involve, and the dangers involved in rushing to celebrate any of its many false dawns, will be explored in the following two chapters. In the closing section of this chapter, I want to give a fuller account of the differences Adorno emphasizes between identity philosophy and the kind of philosophy he seeks to articulate – which is sensible of its own inadequacies in the face of reality – focusing in particular again on what he means by 'dialectic'.

Dialectic, for Adorno, can be reduced neither to thought nor to things: it is in both. Adorno states in the 'Introduction' to *Negative Dialectics* that 'Dialectic is the consistent sense of non-identity. It does not begin by taking a standpoint. My thought is driven to it by its own inevitable insufficiency, by my guilt of what I am thinking' (ND: 5). Dialectic is not a method to be established before any thinking of any thing. Adorno makes clear precisely what this insistence that dialectic is not a standpoint entails at the beginning of his book on Husserl, somewhat unfortunately translated into English as *Against Epistemology: A Metacritique* (the title is more properly translated as *Towards a Metacritique of Epistemology*). He discusses dialectic there in connection with the idea of 'immanent critique', which I explored earlier. The title of the English translation is unfortunate because it betrays the idea of 'immanent critique' that Adorno aims to elaborate in the early pages of the book. Adorno does not set up a position 'against epistemology' but rather pursues its logic 'to where the latter [that is, epistemology] cannot afford to go'. This insistence on pushing logic to its outer limits means that 'Dialectic's very procedure is immanent critique' (ME: 5). Adorno means that dialectic advances arguments to the point at which they themselves are forced to admit their own untruth. It is in this admission of untruth that dialectic finds truth.

Moreover, dialectic is a consciousness that is not simply intellectual but is also a kind of sense, which echoes Adorno's view that thinking cannot decisively be divorced from impulse. On the one hand, the insistence that dialectic is the sense of thought's inadequacy to what it thinks about means that dialectic is, as it were, the revenge of things against thought. 'Dialectic lies in things' (ND: 205). On the behalf of what is subsumed beneath conceptual generalization, 'dialectics is a challenge from below' (ND: 303). On the other hand, Adorno criticizes the kind of dogmatic materialism that would simply take this as a warrant for the arrest of thought. Dialectics, then, 'could not exist without the consciousness that reflects it – no more than it can evaporate into that consciousness' (ND: 205). Indeed, dialectics is as much against things as it is against thought because otherwise it too would lapse into mere affirmation of what exists in opposition to every thought that things might be different. Rather, dialectic emerges and exists in the gap between thought and thing so long as that gap persists. It is not, then, a method of doing philosophy for all time, but critical reflection on antagonism so long as real antagonisms persist. Adorno's view of antagonistic society, and the kinds of contradictions it produces, is the topic of the next chapter.

SUMMARY

The expressive – or, rather, aesthetic – aspect of philosophy is central to Adorno's view of philosophy as such. Philosophy cannot be reduced, for Adorno, to a set of axioms or principles; rather, his emphasis on 'philosophical composition' is meant to suggest that the way a philosophical text or authorship develops is as important as any position that can be extracted from it. Crucial to this kind of view of philosophy are Adorno's ideas of 'immanent criticism' and 'dialectic'. He sees dialectical philosophy in opposition to the kind of positivist philosophy that he views as merely reproducing reality as it is. This intellectual approach is conservative, as are a range of other apparently very different philosophical projects, chiefly that of Heidegger. Dialectic responds to a real situation in which antagonism is rife; it is therefore a response to the antagonistic structure of contemporary society.

5

LIFE DOES NOT LIVE

ADORNO IN AMERICA

'Freedom isn't free.' This statement, usually emblazoned on fridge magnets, bumper stickers and key rings, is a favourite slogan of contemporary American neo-conservatives. From the last line of a piously nationalistic piece of doggerel, it is meant as a sober reminder that the freedoms enjoyed by citizens of Western democracies, especially Americans, have been and continue to be won through considerable expenditure of life, limb and resources. Such a slogan can, of course, lay claim to a certain heritage, from Aristotle to Thomas Jefferson, in which constant vigilance is seen as a necessary condition of freedom. Adorno, however, would have read 'Freedom isn't free' as an unconscious admission that even those societies which most loudly proclaim their love of freedom have yet to achieve it, and, indeed, that they often restrict the freedom of their own citizens and those of other countries, sometimes violently.

It is important to bear in mind from the beginning of this chapter on Adorno's social and moral criticism – especially in view of what I have just said about the unwitting admissions of contemporary American neo-conservatism – that Adorno's writing hardly indulges in the kind of fatuous denunciation of Western societies which have been particularly prevalent since the attacks of 11 September 2001 and the American and British military and legislative responses to them. Naturally enough, Adorno was deeply unhappy to have been displaced from his home in Germany, first to Britain and ultimately to America, during the Second World War. His experience of America was not, however, entirely barren; not least because he was reunited with the other members of the Institute for Social Research, including, in particular, Max Horkheimer. During the early parts of his sojourns, first in New York and the East Coast, then in California, Adorno was especially attentive to the new experience of America's beauty, which lay for him in the fact 'that even the smallest of its segments is inscribed, as its expression, with the immensity of the whole country' (MM: 49). But even Adorno's enjoyment of the American landscape was ultimately qualified:

> It is as if no-one had ever passed their hand over the landscape's hair. It is uncomforted and comfortless. And it is perceived in a corresponding way. For what the hurrying eye has seen merely from the car it cannot retain, and the vanishing landscape leaves no more traces behind than it bears upon itself.
>
> (MM: 48)

This might seem to hint at a wistful Romanticism. The title of the aphorism which concludes with these remarks is, after all, 'Paysage': the French for 'landscape', both in the sense of natural scenery and landscape painting. This is a kind of sullen longing for the decorous gentility of what the former US Defense Secretary Donald Rumsfeld called 'old Europe'. Adorno's homesickness and despair at exile are certainly registered in a passage like this. More importantly, though, such comments also suggest some of his most abiding philosophical concerns – with, for example, the way that perceptions depend on the embodied experience of perceiving subjects, such as the way that a landscape looks different from behind the windscreen of a car, or from the perspective of a worker in a field, or from a viewing-point – and also rely on some of his deepest insights into humanity's relationship with itself and with nature. In this regard and in many others, his American experience fostered some of Adorno's most important philosophical reflections. But while America was a refuge for him, Adorno did not see it as the 'land of the free'.

At least partly out of this fraught, contradictory experience of refuge in America came Adorno's great work of exile, *Minima Moralia*, with which this chapter is largely concerned. Adorno chose as the epigraph for the first part of this book the sentence 'Life does not live', taken from a novel entitled *Der Amerikamüde* (*He who Is Tired of America*), by the nineteenth-century Austrian writer Ferdinand Kürnberger (1821–79). In particular, Adorno seeks to question whether life can simply go on in the wake of the catastrophe of the Second World War, and, more generally, under the shadow of ever more ossified relations of capitalistic exchange. 'One must live with the times,' says Nagg in Beckett's *Endgame*, but part of the point of that play, which I discussed at the end of Chapter 3, is to ask whether life is now anything more than the barest existence. Life itself has been altered by the conditions in which it is lived.

Adorno's sense that 'life does not live' was especially sharpened by his experience of exile, of American society, and of the Second World War. Also fundamental to his diagnosis of what has become of 'life' under contemporary conditions was his early engagement with the work of the Hungarian writer Georg Lukács (1885–1971). Lukács's eventual (although temporary) support for the Stalinist regime in the Soviet Union during the post-war years – and especially his conservatively minded denunciations of Modernist artworks – drew stern criticism from Adorno. The influence of Lukács's books *The Theory of the Novel* and *History and Class Consciousness* on the development of Adorno's thinking, however, can hardly be overestimated. Central to *The Theory of the Novel*, in particular, is the radically pessimistic view that modern existence is devoid of meaning. In Lukács's terms, modern existence has seen the severance of 'life' from 'essence' (Lukács 1971a: 30). Lukács sees in art, and, paradigmatically, in the novel form, the registration of this rupture between life as it is and life as it could be. This is not to say, however, that if we want meaning, we can simply turn to art. Lukács firmly denies the ability of art actually to transform reality: 'it is only a demand and not an effective reality' (Lukács 1971a: 85). As we saw in Chapter 3, this view of art is central to Adorno's thinking.

Lukács's diagnosis of modern consciousness and of the modern view of nature is further developed in his *History and Class Consciousness*, particularly in its lengthy central chapter, 'Reification and the Consciousness of the Proletariat'. The term 'reification' (from the Latin *res* for 'thing') refers to the conversion of a process or relationship into a thing. In particular, developing a thesis of Marx's *Capital*, Lukács uses this term to refer to the way that, in capitalist societies, relations between people have taken on the illusory form of relations between things and, in particular, that the laws of capitalist exchange have hardened into apparently natural laws (Marx 1976: 163–77). Lukács's thesis that this affects both the way in which the real world and the conceiving subject are envisaged became extremely significant to Adorno's work. In particular, the fact that relations between living people have been overtaken by the laws governing the exchange of commodities in capitalist societies means that the importance of 'life' has come to be radically diminished.

Thus, following Marx and Lukács, Adorno contends that capitalist society reduces the human being to the status of worker, which, in turn, is perceived as a commodity. Human labour is saleable and replaceable like any other commodity. This reduction of human life is central to Adorno's view of fascism, with which his account of modern moral and political life is, of course, connected. It is important to note that Adorno saw fascism not as a kind of satanic magic visited upon a previously just and happy society, but rather as the most extreme intensification of tendencies already latent within the capitalistic insistence that anything – human beings included – could in principle be exchanged for anything else. When life has become disposable in this way, it is open to question whether it is really still life at all. The meaning of this question for Adorno's moral theory is one of the central concerns of this chapter.

THE AIM OF *MINIMA MORALIA*

Adorno first started to write down the aphorisms that would constitute *Minima Moralia* during his stay in England, where he was registered as an advanced student at Merton College, Oxford. As in America, Adorno's experience in England involved genuine intellectual achievement as well as straitened circumstances and, in some respects, acute frustration with his academic situation. The immediate damage to Adorno's life – the subtitle of *Minima Moralia* is *Reflections on Damaged Life* – was done by the exile to which he was driven by the triumph of Nazism in Germany and subsequently throughout Europe. This is not at all to say, though, that *Minima Moralia* is merely the autobiography, however reflective, of an individual in which the tumultuous times through which he lived are chronicled. The damage to life that it addresses is much more far reaching than that. To get a proper sense of *Minima Moralia*, we need to consider its aim; or, rather, what its aim would be, were it still possible to achieve it. At the beginning of the 'Dedication' to Horkheimer with which the book opens, Adorno relates the investigation that he presents in the rest of the book to what used to be considered the true field of philosophy: 'the teaching of the good life'.

This essential vocation of philosophy has fallen into abeyance for two connected reasons. The first fault lies with philosophy itself, because philosophy has lapsed into mere method, which is to say – as we saw in the discussion of Adorno's criticisms of various forms of contemporary

MORALIA, MAGNA AND MINIMA

The title, *Minima Moralia*, ironically alludes to an ancient Greek work of moral philosophy, which may or may not have been by Aristotle, entitled *Magna Moralia*. The *Magna Moralia*, like Aristotle's great works in moral philosophy, the *Nicomachean Ethics* and *Eudemian Ethics*, deals with the chief topics in classical Aristotelian ethics, such as moral excellence, happiness, what it is to be good, and the relation between these. The shift from *magna* to *minima*, from 'great' to 'least of all', or 'very little', is meant to register both the disintegration of the philosophical vocation to teach the good life and the decreased possibility for any straightforwardly good life at all under contemporary conditions.

philosophy in the last chapter – that philosophy ties itself to and thus affirms what already exists. The second fault lies with what has become of life itself. 'What the philosophers once knew as life', Adorno remarks, 'has become the sphere of private existence and now of mere consumption, dragged along as an appendage of the process of material production, without autonomy or substance of its own' (MM: 15). Moral questions have come to have secondary importance in the face of economic growth and productivity for their own sakes. In a phrase that has increasing currency in contemporary political debate and in which it is tacitly admitted that 'life' is a luxury in which we might indulge after hours, the 'work–life balance' is desperately off kilter. This means, for Adorno, that moral teaching of the kind developed in traditional philosophy is fatally compromised because what it would teach to be good – 'life' – has itself changed. Individual moral actions take place within a general context of immorality: 'There is no right life in false life' or, as Adorno's translator has it, 'Wrong life cannot be lived rightly' (MM: 39). In an extremely impressive recent account – and attempted reconstruction – of Adorno's ethical theory, J.M. Bernstein assesses the precise significance of private life for Adorno's understanding of the contemporary moral situation. On the one hand, private life can be seen, in the face of universal immorality, as 'a refuge for goodness' (Bernstein 2001: 45). That is, practices of private life, such as love, marriage and dwelling, contain some element of hope for genuine ethical ideals (Bernstein 2001: 44). On the other hand, private life is still contaminated by the general withering of ethical existence. For a start, these practices are 'deformed through being forced to carry (nearly) the full weight of ethical existence and ideality', which is to say both that love, marriage, dwelling and so on cannot simply stand in for the kind of universal ethical life which is felt to be lacking and that, when they are made to perform this substitution, they themselves are put under intolerable stress. Moreover, there is no ultimately decisive division, for Adorno, between private practice and the universal morality for which it is meant to substitute (Bernstein 2001: 45). This is not to say that Adorno's position is a kind of resignation in the face of global immorality, according to which anything goes because nothing can be properly evaluated. His reticence with regard to the traditional aims of moral philosophy is, rather, quite specific, as Bernstein makes clear: 'What is denied is that here and now our actions can be unconditionally good or worthy, uncompromised, not a further abetting of what they mean to resist, and consistent with their own normative presuppositions and insistences' (Bernstein 2001: 57 n. 17). The task of *Minima Moralia*, therefore, is not to offer straightforward guides to right action but to examine the whole context of wrong life so that the very possibility or impossibility of morality might fully be explored.

DIALECTIC OF MORALITY

We can follow Bernstein in taking the statement that 'there is no right life in false life' as a kind of motto for Adorno's considerations of moral philosophy in general. In his lecture course on Problems of Moral Philosophy, delivered in Frankfurt University in 1963 and published posthumously, Adorno returned to the exact meaning of this motto a number of times. His attempts to develop what it means that 'there is no right life in false life' are central to his conception of the 'dialectics of morality', which was, as he emphasized in a number of the lectures, the central focus of the course (e.g., PMP: 158). We saw in Chapter 1, for example, what it means that there is a dialectic of enlightenment; here, we need to set out the way in which, for Adorno, morality is dialectical.

In his earlier lecture series on Kant's *Critique of Pure Reason* (1959), Adorno had focused on Kant's theoretical philosophy, which is to say on that branch of Kant's philosophy aimed at answering the question 'What can I know?' In his lectures on moral philosophy, Kant is again the focus, but this time Adorno turns to his practical philosophy: namely, to Kant's attempt to answer the question 'What must I do?' The key to Kant's moral philosophy is what he calls in the *Groundwork for the Metaphysics of Morals* (1785) the 'categorical imperative' (Kant 1996b: 73). An 'imperative' is the formula of a command, issued by reason to the will, to do something. Imperatives always contain the word 'ought'. An imperative commands 'categorically' when it insists that an action is necessary in itself and not merely as a means to some other end. Categorical imperatives do not tell you that you should do an action because it will make someone else happy, because it will make you look good, because it will make you feel good, or whatever. Although Kant terms it in different ways, the categorical imperative comes down to the rule that you should act only if you can will that the basis on which you act should become a law applicable to all agents at all times (Kant 1996b: 73).

Kant's, therefore, is a fundamentally rationalistic theory of morality, which allows room neither for sentiment nor for consideration of the consequences of actions in the formulation of moral imperatives. However, Adorno argues that where Kant insists most emphatically on the primacy and purity of reason in determining moral action, his theory becomes irrational. This is part of what Adorno means by the dialectics of morality; that is, when rationally conceived moral convictions are most stolidly adhered to, that is when they are most likely to become immoral. In much the same way, where Kant attempts to establish freedom on a solely rational basis, freedom becomes tantamount to unfreedom. Adorno explains the latter point in a way that echoes the kind of argument we encountered in *Dialectic of Enlightenment* about the renunciation of impulse as the basis on which the rational self is founded:

Kant . . . banishes sympathy, compassion and the direct expression of pity from his ethics because all impulses of this sort are merely natural impulses, and are purely instinctual. As such they are said to be incompatible with pure reason, with the principle of reason. Therefore, because this extreme view of the concept of freedom is based on its absolute independence from all existing beings, from nature as such, it threatens to become transformed into unfreedom. Human beings have denial imposed upon them and above all they are not able to recover those things they have been forced by this imperative to renounce.

(PMP: 119–20)

Recent advocates of Kant's moral theory, such as Onora O'Neill, Christine M. Korsgaard and Robert B. Louden, have sought to defend him from comparable types of criticism by pointing to aspects of his authorship that appear to allow for some sort of a morality of compassion and sympathy. Adorno does not attempt this kind of reconstruction of Kant's moral theory but while in the *Problems of Moral Philosophy* he shows only limited interest in anything other than the formalism of Kant's conception of duty according to the categorical imperative, he does not simply seek to condemn as inhuman the consequences of Kant's view. The dialectics of morality is not simply confined to Kant. We can see this clearly in Adorno's discussion of the kind of criticism that Hegel develops of Kant's practical philosophy. Whereas Kant's is an 'ethics of conviction' (that is, a moral theory that views ethical action according to subjective disposition or conviction (*Gesinnung*) concerning what is right, regardless of consequence) Hegel develops an 'ethics of responsibility' (that is, a view which insists that the context for and consequences of particular actions be taken into account). Hegel divides moral theory, or the 'philosophy of right', into abstract right, 'morality' (*Moralität*), and 'ethical life' (*Sittlichkeit*) (Hegel 1991).

In order to draw out the contrast with Kant, we need briefly to focus on the distinction that Hegel establishes between 'morality' and 'ethical life'. On the one hand, the 'moral point of view . . . takes the shape of the *right of the subjective will*' and thus, in a fairly Kantian fashion, emphasizes will and intention (Hegel 1991: 136; see also Inwood 1992: 192). On the other hand, 'ethical life' has 'a fixed content which is necessary for itself, and whose lasting existence is exalted above subjective opinions and preferences: they are *laws and institutions which have being in and for themselves*' (Hegel 1991: 189 [translation modified]; see also Inwood 1992: 92). That is, whereas 'morality', for Hegel, names the realm of individual will and freedom, 'ethical life' refers to action in the context of and mediated by a whole set of traditions, rituals and institutions, such as the family, law, civil society and the state. Importantly, Hegel recognized that these differing versions of right can come into conflict. He does, however, present a reconciliation of these differences in the modern Germanic state, broadly conceived: 'The present has cast off its barbarism and unjust arbitrariness, and truth has cast off its otherworldliness and contingent force, so that the true reconciliation, which reveals the state as the image and actuality of reason, has become objective' (Hegel 1991: 380).

I have only offered, of course, a brief account of Hegel's moral and political philosophy. It is nevertheless already clear that Adorno would not accept the kind of conclusion that Hegel draws. In the wake of the Second World War, it could hardly be said that 'the spiritual realm brings the existence of its heaven down to earth in this world', in however qualified a sense (Hegel 1991: 380). While Adorno rejects the conclusion of Hegel's philosophy of right, he thinks that aspects of its criticism of Kant's practical philosophy are still valid. He equally thinks that aspects of Kant's formalism are a kind of anticipatory criticism of the conservatism inherent in Hegel's position. Adorno attempts to bring out this mutual criticism of the ethics of conviction and the ethics of responsibility through a reading of *The Wild Duck* (1884), a play by the Norwegian playwright Henrik Ibsen (1828–1906) (PMP: 159–64; see also Ibsen 1960). For the purposes of his discussion of how this play illuminates moral philosophy, Adorno is chiefly interested in the character of Gregers Werle and his, as Adorno puts it, 'respect for abstract moral principles' (PMP: 159). According to Adorno, the difficulties into which this leads Werle – and the other characters – demonstrates Adorno's dictum that 'there is no right life in false life'. It does this not only by showing, against Kant, 'how a man becomes immoral simply by defending the moral law' (PMP: 158) but by stating, against Hegel, that

> the really dialectical element lies in the fact that even in this play the ethics of responsibility and the world for which it acts as a sort of apologia are also depicted as so problematic, so bad, and above all so much in collusion with the existing order, that Gregers Werle, who is in the wrong as the advocate of abstract morality, is seen also as being in the right.
>
> (PMP: 162)

There is in the phrase 'the *really* dialectical element' (my emphasis) a trace of that suspicion, discussed in the last chapter, that Hegel's philosophy is not ultimately sufficiently dialectical. In any case, Adorno seeks to distance himself from Hegel's conservatism and to preserve the critical force of the independence of Kant's formalism from things as they are.

WHAT IS 'LIFE'?

We need now to explore in more detail what Adorno sees as the consequences of morality's retreat into private life and to attempt to grasp more precisely what he means by 'life'. One of the chief absurdities that post-war thinking must face, according to Adorno, is that a culture that (at least) had failed to prevent Auschwitz and Hiroshima, and that (at most) had perpetrated them, continues. On his return to Germany, Adorno was extremely critical of any suggestion that business as usual was still possible. Whatever remains of the private existence upon which bourgeois individualism was based is not immune to the catastrophic course of world events, but, rather, is robbed of whatever used to be good in it. Thus, 'privacy has given way to the privation it always secretly was' (MM: 34). Moral theory, then, can hardly be salvaged from the wider immorality of society. There is, for Adorno, no inner core of moral personhood that is not touched by the circumstances in which it finds itself.

It is especially significant, therefore, that when, in *Negative Dialectics*, Adorno wishes to show how 'even concepts abstract enough to seem to approach invariance prove to be historic', he focuses on the concept of 'life' (ND: 262–3). Part of the demonstration of the historical nature of the concept of life involves showing that 'life' is not simply reducible to the biological concept of self-preservation. In contemporary society, which reduces 'life' to a biological category of production and reproduction, subjects are blindly compelled by a process over which they have no control. Were the process of production and reproduction to become transparent to human subjects and were they then able to control it, then the meaning of 'life' would change from something that happens to you to something that you live. Until then, people are dead:

> Only when the process that begins with the metamorphosis of labour-power into a commodity has permeated men through and through and objectified each of their impulses as formally commensurable variations of the exchange relationship, is it possible for life to reproduce itself under the prevailing relations of production. Its consummate organization demands the coordination of people that are dead. The will to live finds itself dependent on the denial of the will to live: self-preservation annuls all life in subjectivity.
>
> (MM: 229)

This crucial passage needs careful unpacking, and some of its central assumptions need to be seen in the light of Adorno's reception of Marx's theory of labour. Marx's project as a whole is a thoroughgoing critique of bourgeois political economy (see Jarvis in Huhn 2004: 87). One of the most important aspects of this critique is his examination of the way that labour is conceived by classical political economists such as Adam Smith and David Ricardo. 'Political economy', comments Marx, in the first of his early 'Economic and Philosophical Manuscripts', 'regards labour abstractly as a thing; labour is a commodity' (Marx 1975: 293). Like all other commodities, labour must find a buyer (Marx 1975: 283). The problem with this identification of labour as a commodity is that it is unlike other commodities: labour is alive. Marx develops an account both of how political economy operates with a reductive view of labour and, most significantly for our purposes here, of how the exclusive focus on the worker *as a worker and nothing else* entails the diminution of life itself, which is thus conceived as the mere ability to perform work. Life becomes a commodity. Setting out this context enables us to see that what Adorno is pointing to here is a dialectic of life; which is to say to the way that, under the thoroughgoing commodification of labour, life takes on the characteristics of, and ultimately turns into, its opposite – namely, death. As I discussed in Chapter 1 in the account of self-preservation in *Dialectic of Enlightenment*, life that lives merely to keep itself alive has really ceased to live in any meaningful sense.

Just because you have a pulse, therefore, does not mean that you are alive. Adorno is concerned to differentiate between what Eric L. Santner (2006: 17, *passim*) has recently defined as 'undeadness' – the barest kind of mere survival – and living. Life will fully be life only in an emancipated world, 'and survival', as Adorno puts it, 'has something nonsensical about it, like dreams in which, having experienced the end of the world, one afterwards crawls from a basement' (MM: 38). This distinction between mere life and living life not only relies on Marx's theory of labour but echoes the division in Christian theology between the infernal existence of the damned and the eternal life of the saved. Most important to the differentiation between dead life and living life that Adorno seeks to elaborate in *Minima Moralia* and elsewhere, however, are Benjamin's reflections on what has become of life and, even more prominently, of experience. Towards the conclusion of his extremely complex and influential argument about the relationship between law and the specific nature of human being in his 'Critique of Violence', Benjamin questions the assumption that life as such is sacred: 'Man cannot, at any price, be said to coincide with the mere life in him, any more than it can be said to coincide with any of his conditions and qualities, including even the uniqueness of his bodily person' (Benjamin 1996b: 251). Giorgio Agamben has discussed at length in his important book *Homo Sacer: Sovereign Power and Bare Life* how Benjamin, along with a number of twentieth-century political thinkers, sought to show that the idea of 'bare' or 'mere' life is associated with the establishment of political power that absolutely holds sway over such life (Agamben 1998: 66). What needs to be emphasized here is Benjamin's suspicion of the valorization of life once it has been reduced to its mere biological component, which is to say to that 'life' which human beings share with plants, animals and gods. Benjamin is focusing on the way that 'life' is stripped of everything that makes it valuable and is then vociferously valued none the less. He develops a connected argument with regard to what has become of 'experience' under modern conditions.

Indeed, one of the most widely debated areas of Benjamin's philosophy is this critique of modern experience and the way in which it was taken up by members of the Frankfurt School, including Adorno. Benjamin's account of experience rests on a distinction, which is difficult to render into English, between *Erfahrung* (experience as a kind of narrative, as the result of the abiding articulation of discrete experiences into a coherent whole) and *Erlebnis* (individual lived experiences, not necessarily made to cohere according to a unifying narrative). In his subtle and insightful book on Benjamin's philosophy of experience, Howard Caygill (1998: 30–3) draws attention to the importance for Benjamin's concept of experience of his short essay 'Experience and Poverty'. In this essay, Benjamin examines the consequences for experience of the kind of warfare newly waged on a grandly mechanized scale in Europe during the First World War. Traditional modes of experience were shattered by the situation into which the newly enfeebled human being was thrust. While this is, for sure, an account of the horrific collapse of narrative, reflected experience, Benjamin is far from condemning all types of new, isolated experience. Indeed, much of his philosophy is dedicated to exploring them in great depth. For Adorno, however, the reduction of 'life' to its barest minimum and the dissolution of experience into the most diffuse fragments has taken on an all-the-more-radical character. Following Benjamin, Adorno remarks, 'Life has changed into a succession of shocks, interspaced with empty, paralysed intervals' (MM: 54). The disarticulation of life into a series of shocks – themselves deathly – allows for the insertion between the shocks of hollow, meaningless existence. Death fills the spaces between the segments of a life cut and spliced.

This description of what has become of 'life' in modern society is connected to important aspects of Adorno's philosophy, particularly with regard to his view of objects and of the conceptual tools with which they are grasped. I discussed in the last chapter how Adorno insists on the non-identity of concept and object. As positivist thought confidently reduces the object to its concept, we have seen here that, for Adorno, contemporary society aims to reduce things to their functions. People are also increasingly reduced to things in order all the more easily to be reduced to their functions within the context of material production. The relation between things and people – in particular the way that attitudes to things come to resemble and influence attitudes to people – is central to Adorno's account of the way that society has become ever more instrumental. Experience itself is reduced to mere function because functional things allow no relationship with them other than use (MM: 40). This is the case, Adorno argues, even with those things given as gifts, which were once supposed to escape the context of mere functionality. In his aphorism 'Articles may not be exchanged', from *Minima Moralia*, Adorno argues that both charitable giving and private giving have been drained of the human impulse that was once essential to them. The former has become another form of administration and 'is necessarily accompanied by humiliation through its distribution, its just allocation, in short through treatment of the recipient as an object' (MM: 42). The latter no longer involves the imagination of the recipient's joy and the careful – or, perhaps better, caring – consideration of what he or she would want that goes with such imagination. The proof of this lies not just in the shelves full of 'gift ideas', already witnessed by Adorno, but in the fact that guests at weddings are nowadays invited to purchase gardening equipment and crockery from a 'gift list' that the happy couple themselves have drafted. Adorno concedes that this kind of procedure would be preferable simply to having to accept a hundred toasters and kettles, but his point is rather to indicate what has been lost in the transition to a more utilitarian view of gift-giving. Indeed, the administration of both charitable and private giving, and the elimination of the human impulse that might be involved in both, has recently come together in the invention of the charitable wedding gift list, whereby the impoverished inhabitants of African villages benefit from your nuptials by receiving a goat. From Adorno's perspective, these tendencies indicate the reduction to mere function of both things and, through their isolation, of people.

DON'T KEEP SMILING

This discussion of charity is attached to Adorno's far-reaching critique of supposedly positive ethical stances and attitudes. In particular, he more broadly adopts aspects of Nietzsche's critique of compassion, while at the same time disavowing various brands of Nietzschean self-affirmation. We need briefly to look at this discussion in order more fully to grasp Adorno's view of the connection – and disconnection – between morality and society. Morality has been confined to private life, which is to say that it has been separated from society; and, shackled to the process of production and reproduction, private life itself has become a shadow of what it might be. Both of these elements of the current moral predicament can already be seen in Adorno's description of what has become of both private and charitable giving. His critique of the latter – 'the planned plastering-over of society's visible sores' (MM: 42) – is echoed by his discussion of compassion. This discussion plays an important part in Adorno's account of moral philosophy. In a way that mirrors his extrapolation of the dialectics of morality out of the relationship between Kant and Hegel, Adorno seeks to mobilize Nietzsche's critique of compassion, while at the same time drawing the precise orientation of that critique into question. Thus, the pity for others inherent in compassion is both preserved and rejected.

Adorno is more clearly suspicious of any straightforward affirmation of life, à la Nietzsche, in response to what is viewed as the moribund nature of contemporary moral life. Indeed, one of the appeals of Kafka's novels for

VITALISM AND 'LIFE-PHILOSOPHY'

Adorno's repudiation of the heroic affirmation of life is part of his general wariness regarding the irrationalist elements in the thinking of writers such as Wilhelm Dilthey (1883–1911), Henri Bergson (1859–1941), Ludwig Klages (1872–1956) and Oswald Spengler (1880–1936), each associated with early twentieth-century 'life-philosophy' (*Lebensphilosophie*). While vitalism, as Herbert Schnädelbach has shown in his important book on *Philosophy in Germany 1831–1933*, reaches at least as far back as the early work of Hegel and the work of Schopenhauer (Schnädelbach 1984: 139–41), one of the most important characteristics of life-philosophy was its interpretation of Nietzsche's philosophy, especially of his early essay 'On the Uses and Disadvantages of History for Life' (Schnädelbach 1984: 62). In that essay Nietzsche placed great emphasis on the need for history to serve the 'vital powers', which themselves were established as a kind of ultimate value (Nietzsche 1983). While it is plausible that Adorno assimilated aspects of life-philosophy, he was nevertheless fiercely and consistently critical of the irrationalism inherent in versions of it, especially because it entailed, at least in the cases of Klages and Spengler, an affinity with fascism.

Adorno is the way in which he sides with death against the deathliness of life. Kafka shows how, 'in a world caught in its own toils, everything positive, every contribution, even the work that reproduces life, helps increase that entanglement' (P: 271). This negation, as opposed to wishful affirmation, is central to the way in which Adorno envisages a moral critique of society. Like the way in which Marx developed his 'Critique of Political Economy' in *Capital* by asking how 'free' the 'free markets' and how 'fair' the 'fair exchange' of capitalist economies really are, critics of society hardly need to invoke moral categories wholly unbeknown to society in order to condemn it, but must rather confront society with its own morality. Thus, for apologists of society as it is, Adorno remarks, there is 'no other defence than to reject the very principle by which society was judged, its own morality' (MM: 93). The concentration camp, the atom bomb and environmental catastrophe lead to the suspicion that bourgeois society would prefer its own destruction to the fulfilment of its very own emancipatory principles.

SUMMARY

Against the background of his experience of exile, Adorno's *Minima Moralia* is an attempt to confront the contemporary impossibility of moral philosophy and, indeed, of moral life itself. Morality has become dialectical because dogged adherence to abstract moral principles can lead to immorality, and an ethical life that focuses on existing institutions and forms of life can easily become a kind of apology for things as they are. Central to Adorno's conception of moral philosophy today is a consideration of what 'life' now is. The attempt to teach the 'good life' is compromised by the fact that 'life' itself has radically altered.

6

PHILOSOPHY, STILL

REALIZATION OF PHILOSOPHY

One of the less violent ways in which inhabitants of the former East Germany were constantly reminded that they were living in a Utopia was by large billboards declaring, alongside the image of a chiselled Karl Marx, '*Seine Ideen haben wir verwirklicht*' ('We have realized his ideas'). That inhabitants of former Eastern Bloc countries needed to be informed that they were living in a society finally fit for humanity by propaganda like this – which clearly echoes Western adverts for car insurance, pet food and the various other goods for sale in the 'free market' – is evidence enough that no such society had been achieved. The failure of the realization (*Verwirklichung*) of philosophy's emancipatory kernel is the situation in which Adorno's great philosophical work, *Negative Dialectics*, finds itself. This situation is most explicitly addressed in the famous opening paragraph of the book's 'Introduction': 'Philosophy, which once seemed obsolete,' Adorno begins, 'keeps itself alive because the moment to realize it was missed' (ND: 3 [translation modified]). This striking claim clearly develops the line of thought inaugurated by *Minima Moralia*'s sense that 'life does not live'. The continued value of philosophy cannot simply be assumed and must be accounted for. In the 'Introduction' to *Negative Dialectics*, Adorno goes on to allude to Marx's well-known comment, in the texts that Engels entitled 'Theses on Feuerbach', that 'The philosophers have only *interpreted* the world, in various ways; the point is to *change* it' (Marx 1975: 423). The precise implications of this saying – which has often served as a stick with which to beat allegedly self-indulgent theorizing – was central to Adorno's thinking from the beginning of his career. He sets out his view of philosophy as, precisely, a kind of interpretation in 'The Actuality of Philosophy'. This view of philosophy-as-interpretation is not simply a rebuttal of Marx's dictum; rather, it involves an attempt to overcome the stark opposition between interpreting the world and changing it. 'The interpretation of given reality and its abolition are connected to each other,' Adorno claims, 'not, of course, in the sense that reality is negated in the concept, but that out of the construction of a configuration of reality the demand for its [reality's] real change always follows promptly' (AP: 129). That is, interpretation has what we might describe as an active – rather than merely passive – and polemical sense, for Adorno. Interpretation views the given world in terms of what the world ought to be. In grasping the discrepancy between how the world is and how it ought to be, interpretation demands change. It is thus that 'When Marx reproached the philosophers, saying that they had only variously interpreted the world, and contraposed to them that the point was to change it, . . . the sentence receives its legitimacy not only out of political praxis, but also out of philosophic theory' (AP: 129). Marx's rebuke does not simply demand the renunciation of philosophy and the leap into activism but, rather, that actual practice must be informed by the most profound insight if it is not to risk blindness. Denunciations of theory on behalf of practice must be stripped of their intimidating menace. No practical change for the better has actually come about in the world, nor is any such change immediately on the horizon. Theory is still required if there is even to be hope that the right practice will replace the wrong one.

All too often, the insistence on practical change has not fulfilled philosophy but has simply called it to a halt. The kind of practice that proclaims its status as the fulfilment of radical ideas bears all the scars it inflicted on the philosophy that it banished. None of this is to say, however, that Adorno simply drops the demand that philosophy be realized. For him, philosophy requires its realization. He further elaborates upon this insistence in the 'Introduction' to *Negative Dialectics*:

> Philosophy would be debasing itself all over again, into a kind of affirmative solace, if it were to fool itself and others about the fact that it must, from without, imbue its objects with whatever moves them from within it. What is waiting in the objects themselves needs such intervention to come to speak, and ultimately every theory that is brought to bear on the phenomena, should

come to rest in the phenomena. In that sense, too, philosophical theory means that its own end lies in its realization.

(ND: 29)

This complex and important passage needs careful unpacking in order to gain some idea of what Adorno means by the 'realization' of philosophy. We have already encountered the ideas which this passage suggests. First of all, there is an important echo here of Adorno's account of the criticism of artworks. In Chapter 3, I demonstrated the importance to Adorno of Benjamin's view that German Romantic philosophers and critics like Schlegel and Novalis held that the truth of the work of art is only consummated, so to speak, in its interpretation. Likewise, in Chapter 4, I showed that while Adorno holds that philosophy should attend to objects rather than merely to their conceptual classification, he also contends that philosophy must be independent of what simply exists if it is not to slip into conservative affirmation of the way that things happen to be. The connotations for philosophy of both of these views are taken up again here. Philosophy, if it is to be philosophy and not mere reiteration of what there is, must wake things from their sleep, as it were, on the basis of its independence from those things as they are. Philosophy enables the rebellion of things against their objectification, which is to say that, from a position qualifiedly outside things as they are, it helps to realize what already lies in things as their potential. This, of course, is their potential to be other than what they are at the moment. This implies a certain view of things – that they are not merely reducible to what they are now – as well as of philosophy, and, importantly, of the relation between things and philosophy. These ideas, some of which we have already touched upon in earlier chapters, are difficult to grasp, not least because of their deliberate opposition both to what Adorno saw as the conservatism of accepted philosophical standards of rigour and to the hasty repudiation of theoretical reflection in radical politics, especially in versions of orthodox Marxist activism. This chapter attempts further to explore what Adorno meant by the realization of philosophy, why philosophy is still necessary, and, with the tentativeness with which Adorno himself approached such questions, what a society in which philosophy has been realized might be like.

RECONCILIATION

The realization of philosophy would not mean, for Adorno, philosophy's final triumph, the comprehension and capture of all things by philosophical reflection. The non-identity of thing and concept is not to be overcome in their identity but in the reconciliation of their difference. Clearly, this view of the realization of philosophy carries over into Adorno's view of a just society not as one in which its members would conform to a centrally imposed set of values – in which they would have to pass something like a 'Britishness test', for example, or to pledge allegiance to the flag – but as one in which 'people could be different without fear . . . . An emancipated society, [therefore,] . . . would not be a unitary state, but the realization of universality in the reconciliation of differences' (MM: 103).

Unlike some other thinkers in whose work the idea of Utopia plays a prominent role, Adorno nowhere attempts to give an emphatic account of what the just society would have to be like. There is no equivalent to Plato's *Republic* or *Laws*, or even More's *Utopia*, in Adorno's authorship. On the contrary, Adorno's utopianism shares the negativity of his philosophy as a whole; it is concerned to grasp as precisely as possible the world as it is, while refusing to believe that what is must be. Of course, this should not blind us to the fact that Adorno does have a great deal to say about reconciliation, redemption and Utopia. What it should alert us to is the fact that he is suspicious of any clear programme for Utopia and is concerned to suggest, rather than to affirm, what the right state of things might be like from our knowledge of what the wrong state of things is. Adorno demurs from the views of Utopia cherished by the more traditional strands of the socialist, social democratic and labour movements. In particular, his suspicion of the establishment of wholesome activities like mountaineering and woodworking as the characteristic undertakings of an emancipated society is brilliantly set out in the final aphorism of the second part of *Minima Moralia*, '*Sur l'eau*' ('On the water', the title of a book about sailing by the French novelist and short-story writer Guy de Maupassant). The only genuine wish, for Adorno, is the most simple – 'that no one shall go hungry any more' – because it confronts the wrong that in a world which could feed its inhabitants many times over, millions starve. Often, more elaborate wishes are derived not from human need but from the kind of human conduct that is enchained to the production of goods. The view that emancipated society would be one in which the capacity for unfettered production would be relentlessly exploited relies on precisely the shackling of life to ever-increasing productivity which emancipation would seek to overcome. From Adorno's point of view, the fact that there are departments of the governments of rich countries called 'International Development' is disquieting in its suggestion that the imperative for 'economic growth' must be rolled out across the globe. The wish to 'Make Trade Fair' is an admirable one if it is another – albeit damagingly less direct – way of saying that no one must be hungry ever again; it is sinister if it means that the whole world must be transformed into a market place first. Liberated society may very well 'grow tired of development and, out of freedom, leave possibilities unused, instead of storming under a confused compulsion to the conquest of strange stars' (MM: 156–7).

As well as questioning the tendency to see Utopia as a condition in which all human productive capacities would necessarily be maximized – a view which, in Marx's words, would still belong 'to a social formation in which the process of production has mastery over man, instead of the opposite' (Marx 1976: 175) – this statement also implies an important consideration of what the relationship would be between truly achieved happiness and knowledge. This view is significant because it suggests that total happiness and total knowledge are not the same thing. This is what Adorno suggests when he states that an emancipated society would not be compelled 'to the conquest of strange stars'. Moreover, there is very clearly a certain freedom from contemplation in Adorno's suggestion of what emancipation might involve. '*Rien faire comme une bête* [to do nothing, like a beast], lying on water and looking peacefully at the sky, "being, nothing else, without any further definition and fulfilment", might take the place of process, act, satisfaction' (MM: 157). The ideals of the acquisition of ever-greater knowledge along with the perpetual increase of productivity are questioned. Members of an emancipated society would no longer feel the need to kill time. Liberated human beings would be able to bear silence. The discrepancy between knowledge and happiness hinted at here is more fully explored in a brief paragraph from another of *Minima Moralia*'s aphorisms:

> To happiness the same applies as to truth: one does not have it, but is in it. Indeed, happiness is nothing other than being encompassed, an after-image of the original shelter within the mother. But for this reason no-one who is happy can know that he is so. To see happiness, he would have to pass out of it: to be as if already born. He who says he is happy lies, and in invoking happiness, sins against it. He alone keeps faith who says: I was happy. The only relation of consciousness to happiness is gratitude: in which lies its incomparable dignity.

(MM: 112)

The argument in this paragraph is evidence of a number of important strands in Adorno's thinking. I discussed earlier his suspicion of the wish to 'get something out of' artworks and his connected rejection of the idea that truth is a possession. Even happiness, according to the kind of view that Adorno combats, becomes a commodity. Adorno gestures here at a quite different view of happiness, associated, again, with Benjamin's view of truth – 'The proper approach to [truth] is not . . . one of intention and knowledge, but rather a total immersion and absorption in it' (Benjamin 1998: 36) – and with the psychoanalytic description of happiness in terms of the 'oceanic feeling' of security in the mother's womb. Both Benjamin's concept of truth and, more clearly still, Adorno's concept of happiness in the above passage owe a great deal to Judaeo-Christian accounts both of the fall from blessedness and of redemption. In the Garden of Eden prior to their temptation by Satan, Adam and Eve are good not by virtue of their unfaltering observance of strict codes of moral conduct such as the Ten Commandments – which are handed down to humanity only after the fall from grace – but simply by being. In Eden, what is exists in a state of reconciliation with what is good. God declares His creation good in the opening verses of Genesis not because it conforms with a moral checklist that He has at the back of His mind, but just because it is. There is no rupture between what a thing ought to be and what it is.

Adorno develops aspects of the Judaeo-Christian vision of redemption in addition to the way in which he takes over the biblical view of the separation of happiness from knowledge. Nowhere is this tendency in his thinking more striking than in the final pages of *Minima Moralia*, especially in the much-discussed last aphorism, 'Finale' (*Zum Ende*). We can get a firmer grip on the significance of this closing aphorism by setting it in the context of what, precisely, Adorno takes from the Judaeo-Christian vision of redemption. He holds that thinking cannot finally be separated off from impulse which is, ultimately, physical. He is confirmed in this view by theological accounts of the redemption of the dead. The great religions, Adorno notes, have either maintained a silence about the redemption of the dead or have taught the resurrection of the flesh. He comments approvingly that this shows that 'They take the inseparability of the spiritual and physical seriously' (MM: 242). In this, the theological wish is much closer to a materialist vision of redemption than might have been thought, and is certainly closer to a plausible view of redemption than the claim in an apparently more philosophical idealism that the spirit is everything. 'At its most materialistic, materialism comes to agree with theology. Its great desire would be the resurrection of the flesh, a desire utterly foreign to idealism, the realm of the absolute spirit' (ND: 207). This might be taken to suggest that Adorno's work is indebted to theology in such a way that it is ultimately and inescapably reliant on theological categories. Theologians keen to appropriate Adorno's work for a theological revival robust enough to withstand materialist criticism have put this argument persuasively.

But despite his inheritance of various motifs from the Judaeo-Christian tradition, Adorno frequently has a lot to say against God. As Robert Hullot-Kentor (2006: 199–201) has insightfully argued, Adorno's philosophy – while full of theology – is far from theological. This apparently super-subtle distinction is crucial to a proper understanding of this important aspect of Adorno's work. It is not, Hullot-Kentor emphasizes, that Adorno's philosophy is transformed into theology. Rather, Adorno wishes to preserve for philosophy the theological hope, crucially stripped of its magical mischief, for another world better than this. It is in this way that Adorno 'wanted to conjure the image of divine light not to behold the deity as its source above, but to illuminate the damaged nature below' (Hullot-Kentor 2006: 200).

FAILURE OF REDEMPTION; SURVIVAL OF PHILOSOPHY

Redemption is not guaranteed to humanity. It is important to emphasize here that Adorno's talk of the redemption of *humanity* is to be taken seriously: his view of redemption is indelibly universal. There would be no reprobate left behind, no salvation for the elect, while the rest remain in hell. Adorno was fond of quoting Benjamin's dictum that while there is one beggar left, there is still myth. Central to what might be characterized as Adorno's pessimistic attitude to the possibility of redemption is not just his general experience of the world as in some radical sense wrong, but his witnessing of the specific miscarriage of emancipatory politics at crucial points during his life.

STALIN AND THE USSR

While Adorno was a young man during the ultimately unsuccessful German Revolution of 1918, the specific failure of revolutionary hopes that had the greatest impact on him was that represented by the slide of the Soviet Union into dictatorship. Whatever revolutionary hope might still have remained after the overthrow of the tyrannical tsarist regime by the Russian Revolution of 1917 was dissipated once Joseph Stalin (1879–1953) gradually took control after the death of the revolutionary leader, Vladimir Lenin (1870–1924). Stalin's purges of even the most mildly dissenting voices swept through every branch of Soviet society. Not only did this indicate a ruthless suppression of open debate; it also had dire consequences for the day-to-day functioning of the massive Russian state as large numbers of skilled workers and civil servants were exiled (Kennedy 1989: 418–19). Stalin's tyranny reached its spectacular peak in the so-called Moscow show-trials. In these trials, Stalin's perceived opponents were forced to confess to various outlandish conspiracies largely cooked up in the leader's own paranoid imagination. Adorno was critical of Western apologists for Stalin's methods, emphasizing instead that the achievement of emancipation involves more than simply declaring that Utopia has arrived.

Although politics that aim for the revolutionary change of the world – rather than tweaking bits of it here and there – were much less prevalent in the final decades of the twentieth century and are so today, there are still depressingly many examples of the failure of emancipatory promises. Indeed, the fall of the Berlin Wall itself in 1989 seemed to promise that the world would no longer be divided into power blocs waging war against each other through their minions around the globe, and that the huge resources devoted to the arms race would be diverted to more worthwhile ends. This has hardly materialized.

This pessimism is not, however, reason to give up. Adorno's bleak view of attempts to change the world thus far does not go along with the assumption that because human beings have yet to escape social antagonism, such antagonism is therefore natural and essential. Although Adorno's work hardly contains a programme for revolutionary action, it clearly does contain the wish for deliverance. His philosophy, echoing what he admired in Bloch (NL I: 214–15), refuses to be bowed into accepting that hell is everlasting. For Adorno, as for Bloch (2000: 149), 'there is another truth than the truth of what exists now'. Philosophy continues, both in the hope that things might be different than they are and, particularly, in response to the desperate situation in which the world perpetuates itself. 'The undiminished persistence of suffering, fear and menace', remarks Adorno in 'Why Still Philosophy', 'necessitates that the thought that cannot be realized should not be discarded' (CM: 14).

Adorno is keen to emphasize that this does not mean philosophy can get on with its job without so much as looking up from its desk. Because it has emerged that philosophy neither straightforwardly corresponds to reality nor that its realization is imminent, it is compelled to consider its very purpose. Philosophy must criticize itself. This idea of the self-critique of philosophy is not original to Adorno. The tradition of modern German philosophy began with the 'critical turn' taken by Kant's *Critique of Pure Reason*. The title of Kant's book already indicates its intention to scrutinize the limits of viable knowledge as such. For Adorno, because it is compelled to criticize itself thanks to the failure of its realization, philosophy's self-critical imperative is now specifically historically motivated. This means not only that the lack of reconciliation between thought and thing has not necessarily been around for all time but that it might finally be overcome in reconciliation. We can get a firmer sense of what this might mean if we examine an aspect of Adorno's consideration of why traditional philosophical questions – with which *Negative Dialectics* is full – remain pertinent. In the section on 'Freedom' at the beginning of the third part of *Negative Dialectics*, Adorno addresses a question that we are more likely to find formulated in Hobbes and Locke than in Heidegger and Husserl:

> Reflections on freedom and determinism sound archaic, as though dating from the early times of the revolutionary bourgeoisie. But that freedom grows obsolete without having been realized – this is not a fatality to be accepted; it is fatality which resistance must clarify. Not the least of the reasons why the idea of freedom lost its power over people is that from the outset it was conceived so abstractly and subjectively that the objective social trends found it easy to bury.

> (ND: 215)

Adorno is arguing here that the question of the relationship between freedom and determinism remains relevant even though it seems outdated because freedom was never realized (the term Adorno uses is, again, *verwircklicht*). This approach was central to Adorno's philosophy from the very beginning of his career. In *Dialectic of Enlightenment*, for instance, Adorno and Horkheimer reignite what can look like a lot of old philosophy because that philosophy was never realized as it demanded, but was simply buried. Moreover, this comment on freedom and determinism is significant because it echoes Adorno's sense that there is a certain resistance to the prevailing way things are in thinking itself. I want now, in the final section of this chapter, to consider this idea more fully.

THOUGHT AND FREEDOM

As I outlined earlier, Adorno is resistant to the kind of bourgeois consciousness that would reduce happiness to a possession. As with happiness, so with intelligence: 'A person's intelligence or education is ranked among the qualities that make him suitable for inviting or marrying, like good horsemanship, love of nature, charm, or a faultlessly fitting dinner-jacket' (MM: 188). Intelligence and education are like stocks and shares. It does not matter about the content of intelligence as long as you have it and it yields a high rate of return, such as a good marriage or invitations to the best parties. As soon as intelligence is more than an inert characteristic, it is suspected. 'They bluntly justify their own hostility to mind,' Adorno remarks, 'sensing subversion – not even wrongly – in thought itself, in its independence of anything given, existent' (MM: 188).

The truth in this resistance to thinking is in its recognition that thought involves freedom from prevailing conditions. 'It is incumbent upon philosophy', as Adorno comments in his own attempt to answer the question 'Why Still Philosophy', '. . . to provide a refuge for freedom' (CM: 10). There is, therefore, freedom in thought. There is also, importantly, thought in freedom. 'Freedom means criticism and transformation of situations, not their confirmation through decision within their coercive structure' (ND: 226 [translation modified]). In this statement, the role of criticism should not be underestimated. The point that freedom implies criticism is echoed in Adorno's argument that a genuinely emancipated practice requires theory. As I emphasized at the beginning of this chapter, this is perhaps the fundamental aspect of the response in *Negative Dialectics* to the failure of the realization of philosophy and, moreover, to attempts over-hastily to assert the necessity of practical measures at the expense of further reflection. The insistence on the unity of theory and practice has in fact led, Adorno charges, to the subservience of theory to practice, on the one hand, and to the intellectual emptiness of practice, on the other. Practice shorn of its conceptuality becomes the mere exercise of power. This, of course, is the kind of practice from which the realization of philosophy was meant to free humanity. Not only does theory thus lose out in its rough and ready yoking to practice, but practice too is betrayed. For these reasons, Adorno is suspicious of any attempt to label theory as outdated, as merely engaging in old debates, when there are new battles to be fought. Theory is dismissed as obsolete precisely because its failure still to be realized is painful.

This defence of theory – of why there should still be philosophy when practical matters call so urgently for change – is a central part of the tumultuous and traumatic events of Adorno's final years. In a short but

STUDENT MOVEMENT

The late 1960s saw a remarkable upsurge in agitation by well-organized student movements against the specific atrocities of the Vietnam War and the more generally conceived failings of Western governments. While Adorno did express his opposition to the American involvement in Vietnam, and while he did remain highly sceptical of claims that Western democracy represented the best of all possible worlds, he was extremely suspicious of the flamboyant political rhetoric of various figures associated with the student movements at Frankfurt and elsewhere. This suspicion was very much a continuation of his overall criticism of apologists for Soviet communism, as well as a justified fear that some of the tactics adopted by members of the student movement threatened aspects of academic freedom in particular and intellectual and civic freedoms more generally. The relationship between Adorno and the student movement became increasingly fraught: the Institute for Social Research was occupied by graduate students (Adorno called the police to have them removed) and, on another occasion, one of Adorno's lectures was interrupted by two students. To escape this environment, Adorno went to his habitual holiday destination of Zermatt in Switzerland, near where he died from a heart attack. In her grief, Adorno's widow, Gretel, claimed that the students were responsible for his death.

important article entitled 'Resignation', Adorno attempted to respond to some of the charges of self-indulgent theorizing which were levelled against him by members of the supposedly radical student movements. In this article, Adorno again returns to Marx's much-invoked eleventh thesis on Feuerbach. He notes that Marx's repudiation of the very criticism upon which he had insisted in his youth was inspired by the kind of possibility of imminent change that is wholly invisible today. In the event, the European revolution of 1848 for which Marx had high hopes did not succeed; moreover, the scorn for theory in the Soviet Union allowed repression to become more deeply entrenched. 'The only criticism still tolerated was that people were still not working hard enough' (CI: 200). The prospects for the unity of theory and practice, in which theory is always in fact subordinated to practice, are hardly bright.

Were Adorno to leave his response to the charge of resignation there – with his bleak vision of practical attempts to emancipate humanity – it would not, of course, be anything like decisive. At least, the counter-response would go, we tried. Theory is still resigned, afraid of action, whether its success is guaranteed or not. Adorno anticipates this claim and furthers his argument by accusing the leap to action itself of resignation. Subscribing to a collective programme of action because something must be done shields the party member from consciousness of his impotence. Theory, 'unconfused thinking', is opposed to this. Rather, as Adorno's insistence on the difference of thinking from what already merely exists entails, thinking is tantamount to resistance much more clearly than is signing up to a common cause from which thinking has been banished or, at best, to which thinking is made subservient. Thinking refuses to be satisfied, but, precisely as 'melancholy science', it enters into the outer halls, at least, of happiness: 'thought is happiness, even where unhappiness prevails; thought achieves happiness in the expression of unhappiness. Whoever refuses to permit this thought to be taken from him has not resigned' (CI: 203).

SUMMARY

Although Adorno is highly sceptical of societies that present themselves as having realized the demand for freedom made in philosophy, he still views philosophy as indeed demanding its realization. Crucially, he questions the more traditional ideas of Utopia adhered to in the socialist and labour movements, instead insisting on the tentativeness with which any idea of emancipated society must be approached. Most significant of all, Adorno saw unconstrained and clear thinking as itself a kind of freedom in opposition to those strands of self-proclaimed radical politics that sought to dismiss theory because of the supposed need for immediate practice.

AFTER ADORNO

In melancholic mood after the departure of a promising young academic from the Institute for Social Research, Adorno wrote to Horkheimer that it had become clear 'that after us, strictly speaking, there will be nothing' (quoted in Müller-Doohm 2005: 372). The chirpy response to this gloom – surely requisite at the beginning of a chapter entitled 'After Adorno' – that Adorno did have and continues to have a very great influence on subsequent generations of thinkers is both true and false. On the one hand, his impact on aesthetic and literary theory in particular, and on philosophy and social theory more generally, has certainly been far reaching. Recent work in literary studies and art criticism, for example, has discussed Adorno in connection with a very broad range of material. He also remains significant for the more theoretically informed elements of contemporary radical politics. On the other hand, Adorno's star has not always been quite so high in the firmament as it is now. For instance, he was long best known in English-speaking countries for his empirical social research and especially as a contributor to *Studies in the Authoritarian Personality*, while his major philosophical and literary critical works were virtually ignored. Certain parts of his authorship are still viewed with suspicion. An English composer, for example, recently told me that Adorno's music criticism should be locked away in a cupboard, which testifies to the broader wariness with which his music criticism and musicology are sometimes treated.

Most significantly, the interpretation of Adorno's work within the specific setting of the Institute for Social Research has often been quite critical. Nevertheless, the work of later generations of Critical Theorists, such as Axel Honneth (b. 1949 and the current director of the Institute for Social Research), Albrecht Wellmer (b. 1933) and, in particular, Jürgen Habermas (b. 1929), is unimaginable without the influence of Adorno's thought. (Often when their work is discussed, members of the Institute for Social Research after Adorno's time are divided into second- and third- (and perhaps now even fourth-) generation Frankfurt School theorists. For simplicity's sake, I will refer to them all as belonging either to the 'second' or merely 'subsequent' generation of Critical Theorists in what follows.)

The first part of this chapter – which aims to give a sense of the most significant currents of interpretation of Adorno's work – briefly sets out some of the main features of the criticisms of Adorno advanced by Habermas, Honneth and Wellmer. I then indicate ways in which the initial generation of Frankfurt School theorists – Adorno, of course, in particular – has been defended against these criticisms. I then briefly set out the way in which Adorno's statements on the role of culture after the Holocaust have been taken up in contemporary cultural and literary studies. Finally, I discuss a small selection of work which draws on Adorno in contemporary literary and art criticism. The following 'Further Reading' chapter gives details of specific texts that have been especially influential in the reception of Adorno's thought, along with the details of books that will be helpful for your own further engagement with his work.

ADORNO'S RELEVANCE

Jürgen Habermas was a graduate student of Adorno's at Frankfurt University; he has become one of the most important interpreters of his former teacher's work and, indeed, one of the most significant living philosophers. Despite the profound importance of Adorno to Habermas's development, the latter's work, and the work of Honneth and Wellmer, is clearly conceived as a departure from central aspects of Adorno's thinking. In particular, subsequent generations of Critical Theorists dissent from what is cast as Adorno's overly pessimistic attitude to reason. Habermas, for instance, emphasizes this allegedly undue pessimism both in his reading of *Dialectic of Enlightenment* in one of the pivotal chapters of his *The Philosophical Discourse of Modernity* (1985) and in his attempt throughout his work to elaborate a social theory that will not succumb to those problems which are seen to damage Adorno's thinking.

Habermas charges that *Dialectic of Enlightenment* does not do justice to the progressive potential latent within modern rationality. Adorno and Horkheimer's pessimism with regard to modern reason, Habermas contends, is due to their one-sided view of it. In his voluminous *The Theory of Communicative Action* (1981), Habermas rebukes Adorno and Horkheimer for having failed to pursue 'the inner logics of different complexes of rationality' (Habermas 1984: 382). That is, in particular, Adorno and Horkheimer do not value highly enough the potential of the division between knowledge, morals and taste. This is a significant revision of Adorno's wariness regarding the separation between, for example, aesthetics and other aspects of philosophy. The development of 'expert cultures' – that is, of specialized areas of rationality with their own criteria – allows for, according to Habermas, a kind of series of refuges for rationality that protect reason from power, shielding it from the destruction of critical capacities (Habermas 1987: 113). At the centre of modern culture, for Habermas, is not the triumph of power over reason but rather a vigorous competition between them.

Habermas's critique of Adorno and Horkheimer has been developed in a number of directions. Most importantly, Adorno has been cast as incapable of providing any account of social action. It is charged that social action, for Adorno, is merely mechanical. Helmut Dubiel (b. 1946), another figure closely associated with the development of Critical Theory after Adorno, has expressed this charge in an essay that ostensibly wishes to reconcile first- and second-generation Critical Theory, but which clearly attempts to do so on, and in, the latter's terms:

> The 'earlier' and undeniably more radical version of critical theory explained only the conformist behavior of individuals. According to its conception, the actual driving forces of historical processes are not acting collectives but institutional facts or functional imperatives to which such collectives merely respond mechanically . . . Between the utopian idealism of the theory and the radical negativity of its empirical descriptions, the chance for making the theory relevant to what actual collective actors are planning to do is lost.
>
> (Dubiel 1992: 13)

The real condition of society and of agents within it goes missing, Dubiel argues, in the enormous gulf between Adorno and Horkheimer's elevated hopes and their low estimation of the rational potential of contemporary society.

Honneth, building upon Habermas's critique of earlier Critical Theory, has similarly argued that this alleged underelaboration and underestimation of rationality entails the irrelevance of Adorno's thought for social theory. In particular, neither social opposition nor resistance to prevailing social trends can be accounted for from Adorno's 'despairing perspective' because he can give no indication of the ways in which society itself contains the resources for its improvement (Honneth 1991: 37). For Honneth, the view of society displayed in Adorno and Horkheimer is reductive because it is based on their model of the domination of nature. This has the consequence, moreover, that they can conceive of only those types of social domination that are based on direct or indirect force, and have no room for an account of how it might be possible that 'social groups actively participate in the integration of society' (Honneth 1991: 100). As in Habermas, this conclusion is viewed by Honneth as the result of a reduced view of reason, which, rather than seeing instrumental rationality as one part of rationality more broadly conceived, instead generalizes it, so that instrumental rationality becomes the form of rationality operative in society as such. For Honneth, this means that the work of Adorno and Horkheimer must be superseded if the demand of contemporary Critical Theory is to be fulfilled:

> A central problem for a critical social theory today is thus the question of how the conceptual framework of an analysis has to be laid out so that it is able to comprehend both the structures of social domination and the social resource for its practical overcoming.
>
> (Honneth 1991: xiv)

One of the main aims of Critical Theory after Adorno has been to outline how the work of Adorno and Horkheimer might be modified – sometimes very radically – in order to allow for this kind of account of the 'social resource' for the overcoming of unjust social arrangements. Chief among these modifications is the adoption of the perspective of linguistic philosophy in favour of Adorno's alleged reliance on the philosophy of consciousness; which is to say that rather than basing social theory on the model of 'a subject that represents objects and toils with them', it should rather be based on the perspective of 'intersubjective understanding and communication' (Habermas 1984: 390). Habermas, along with Honneth and Wellmer, takes this move as allowing for the renewal of certain aspects of social theory disavowed by

Adorno and for the abandonment of other aspects cherished by him. Thus, social theory – its attention focused on social interaction, however imperfect, rather than on domination conceived according to the instrumental relation to nature – can point to the resources available within rationality for contributions to social justice. Moreover, this means that Adorno's alleged reliance on a kind of apocalyptic theology, about which Wellmer in particular appears to be embarrassed, can be dropped: 'There is no need for messianic hope in order to make [the feeble traces of a better reason that are contained within bad reason] visible' (Wellmer 1991: 85).

This has been a brisk tour through the development of Critical Theory after Adorno. New work by those figures discussed here continues to appear, and the programme of the Institute for Social Research continues to develop in a number of directions. A more thorough overview of the subsequent development of Critical Theory than it has been possible to give here would have to examine the work of a large number of German- and English-speaking writers.

It should be emphasized, however, that the objections to Adorno inspired, in particular, by Habermas have in turn been subjected to sustained criticism by a number of commentators on Adorno's work. Indeed, this is one feature of the most important recent Anglophone commentary on Adorno. A central emphasis of Simon Jarvis's work on Adorno, for example, is that once the apparently embarrassing and outdated excrescences of his authorship have been set to one side – as often occurs in second-generation Frankfurt School interpretation of his work – then the distinctive value of his authorship also goes missing (Jarvis in Huhn 2004: 79–100). In particular, Habermas is cast as having recognized only half (at most) of the emancipatory thrust of Adorno's work. While Habermas wants to lay much greater emphasis on the rational potential of modern culture, he fails, Jarvis charges, to provide a fully developed account of the fetters that bind the individual subject (Jarvis 1998: 221). An appeal to intersubjective reason that has not fully come to grips with the sacrifice of human nature within the subject itself has failed to learn a central lesson of Adorno's thought.

Jarvis's defence of Adorno is influenced and echoed by J.M. Bernstein and the late Gillian Rose, in particular. As we saw in Chapter 5, a central part of Bernstein's project has been to exploit the resources for ethics – that is, for the recovery of ethical life – to be found in Adorno's work. In particular, Bernstein seeks to extend Adorno's ethical thought so as to allow space for a renewed ethics of compassion at the centre of which is 'a conception of ourselves as injured and injurable animals' (Bernstein 2001: 38). This attempt is clearly at least in part conceived in response to the allegation of flaws in Adorno's thought made by subsequent generations of the Frankfurt School, as Bernstein's earlier work, *Recovering Ethical Life: Jürgen Habermas and the Future of Critical Theory* (1995), clearly demonstrates. Indeed, this recent and more serious consideration of the political and moral significance of Adorno has been further developed in a number of places, including in a special issue of the journal *New German Critique*, edited by Christina Gerhardt, on 'Adorno and Ethics' (Gerhardt 2006), and in Espen Hammer's recent (2006) study of *Adorno and the Political*. As well as giving an extremely thorough account and interpretation of Adorno's political philosophy, Hammer usefully contributes to the counter-criticism of Habermas's view of Adorno. In particular, Habermas's account of two versions of reason, one according to which agents treat each other as mutually accountable being in competition with another according to which they treat each other as objects is cast as falling back behind Adorno's account of the dialectic of rationality. That is, Hammer explains, Habermas 'fails to recognize the intricate ways in which these two attitudes are mutually entangled in a dialectic that, under current conditions, has no obvious resolution' (Hammer 2006: 151). Habermas sees different versions of reason in competition with each other. They are not thereby mutually implicated. From Adorno's perspective, this kind of view overlooks the dialectical involvement of versions of reason with each other.

RESPONSE TO DESPAIR

As we have seen, one of the main complaints against Adorno's philosophy is that it is unduly despairing. I have briefly set out some of the responses to this kind of complaint. But perhaps Adorno's most wide-ranging influence has been precisely through his expressions of apparent despair at the Nazi genocide of European Jews.

These expressions have had an enormous impact on the discussion of what the critic Michael Rothberg, in his book *Traumatic Realism* (2000), has called 'the demands of holocaust representation'. Rothberg lays great stress on the influence of Adorno's dictum that 'to write poetry after Auschwitz is barbaric' (Rothberg 2000: esp. 25, 56; see also P: 34). Rothberg's analysis of this influence is valuable because it draws attention to the various inter-pretations of what Adorno meant by this comment. In order to correct what he casts as the many misapplications of Adorno's remark, Rothberg offers a reading of Adorno's understanding of the possibility and status of poetry after Auschwitz in which two features of his view are taken to be decisive. First, Rothberg draws on Adorno's statement in *Negative Dialectics* that Hitler has imposed on humanity the new categorical imperative that Auschwitz must not be repeated (Rothberg 2000: 49; see also ND: 365). This insistence that the Holocaust must be prevented from happening again means that at the centre of Adorno's interpretation of the disaster of the Nazi genocide is 'the necessity of a new relationship to the future' (Rothberg 2000: 32) Second, Rothberg (2000: 39) emphasizes what he calls the 'dual theory of poetry in Adorno'. He means by this that Adorno certainly condemns the barbarity of art that would '[reproduce] the harmonious narrative of traditional realist forms' while, on the other hand, he insists that art should '[express] the rifts that realist mimesis represses'. This suggests that it is open to art 'to remain true to suffering' (Rothberg 2000: 40).

By establishing the broader philosophical context for Adorno's comments on poetry after Auschwitz, Rothberg is able to point to the misreadings implicit in prominent examples of the reception of this aspect of Adorno's thought. He focuses on an influential essay by the eminent literary critic and philosopher George Steiner (1967) and on a detailed study of post-war German cinema by the scholar of modern German culture Eric L. Santner (1990). It is one of the strengths of Rothberg's account that he does not simply scorn what he casts as these misappropriations of Adorno; rather, he seeks to show that these important instances of the adoption of Adorno's thought differ from Adorno's own understanding of the status of art after Auschwitz.

In Steiner's account, for instance, the central contention is that Auschwitz was possible only at the expense of bourgeois values and culture. Whereas Adorno emphasizes that the Holocaust was a catastrophic intensification of tendencies inherent in Western culture and that it necessitates a renewed attitude to the future, Steiner mourns the passing of an idealistically conceived culture and is, therefore, nostalgic for it (Rothberg 2000: 31–2). In Steiner's appropriation, Rothberg argues, Adorno's thinking about Auschwitz has been directed towards the past.

In comparison to Steiner's glorification of bourgeois culture, Santner posits the Holocaust as a radical and ineluctable break with whatever came before. The affirmation of this kind of break, made by postmodernists like Santner, reveals a hidden similarity with Steiner's yearning for a lost past. What both assume is 'a positive vision of an alternative that has existed or does exist' (Rothberg 2000: 33). Both also assume, of course, that the Holocaust announces a radical break with modernity, which either puts this affirmative alternative at an unbridgeable distance or inaugurates it. Adorno's comments on culture after Auschwitz suggest that he would have supported neither of these positions. First, his view of reconciliation is negative: it does not permit any explicit formulation of what an emancipated society, finally free of the possibility of genocidal catastrophe would be like. Second, Adorno is not so confident that Auschwitz has resulted in a radical break with the conditions that led to it. It cannot decisively be said, Adorno thinks, that those conditions no longer obtain.

I have concentrated on Rothberg's discussion of Adorno's influence on interpretation of 'culture in the wake of catastrophe' to this extent both because it shows how influential Adorno has been and because it demonstrates some of the ways in which subsequent interpretation has altered and, indeed, misread Adorno's thinking. We can take Rothberg's return to the detail of Adorno's work as an example of a much broader attempt in contemporary commentary to question some of the predominant tendencies evident in the earlier reception of Adorno in literary studies and in Anglophone interpretation of continental philosophy. In particular, the earlier adoption and adaptation of Adorno's work by the British literary critic and theorist Terry Eagleton, in his *The Ideology of the Aesthetic* (1990), and, especially, by the American literary and cultural theorist Fredric Jameson, in his *Late Marxism* (1990), have been subjected to recent penetrating scrutiny. Robert Hullot-Kentor has articulated perhaps the most vigorous objections to Jameson's interpretation of Adorno. He castigates Jameson's distance from the details and nuances of Adorno's texts and subjects Jameson's own reconstruction of Adorno into a saleable commodity – Adorno 'may turn out to be just what we need today' (Jameson 1990 quoted in Hullot-Kentor 2006: 227) – to the kind of close analysis that is seen to be lacking in Jameson's account of Adorno. In particular, Jameson is cast as radically out of sympathy with the mode of Adorno's thought. For Jameson, on Hullot-Kentor's account, what cannot easily be grasped is to be cast aside, once its mere mention has given the lustre of glamorous incomprehensibility to the self-promoting censor (Hullot-Kentor 2006: 229).

This kind of suspicion of the view of Adorno which prevailed in earlier English-speaking literary criticism and theory is shared by Robert Kaufman, whose long and exacting study 'Red Kant' is, in part, an account of Jameson's reading of Adorno's reading of Kant (Kaufman 2000a). In this important essay, Kaufman attempts a thoroughgoing renewal of aesthetic theory. He takes Jameson's view of Adorno, and particularly of Adorno's reception of Kantian aesthetics (Kaufman 2000: 707), to be emblematic of a prevalent tendency in Anglophone literary criticism and theory according to which aesthetics is viewed as somehow ideologically compromised; which is to say as somehow concealing false assumptions about the human subject, society, production and consumption which nevertheless serve the interests of a particular social group. This account of Jameson is part of a broader project associated with Kaufman – and, in different ways, with a number of other figures, including Jarvis and Bernstein, as well – to rehabilitate aesthetics after the assault upon it, or neglect of it, by self-proclaimed ideology-criticism. Earlier commentary on Adorno, the implication is, attempted to establish him in the pantheon of literary theorists, whereas, in fact, Adorno's work does not provide any easily recognizable method for approaching artworks; that is, it is hard to extract from it some set of criteria for judging, in particular, works of literature that would add up to a 'literary theory'. Rather, Adorno's work on literature is much more the work of a philo-sophically informed critic (Jarvis 1998: 138).

Two important qualifications should be introduced here. First, this rein-vigoration of aesthetics inspired by a reading of Adorno to which his reception of classical philosophical aesthetics is central does not entail unconcern for the social and political aspect of Adorno's interest in art. The purpose of this kind of return to Adorno's aesthetic theory – and demonstration of the fallacious recruitment of Adorno to the cause of straightforwardly political readings of the aesthetic that goes along with it – is rather to recognize the expression of that import precisely in Adorno's conception of the artwork's negative relation to the world as it is currently – wrongly – constituted.

Second, the description of Adorno as a kind of philosophical critic does not mean that his only value for literary and cultural studies is in those commentaries he wrote himself on specific authors and artists. Although Adorno's engagement with art insists on the criticism of particular works and bodies of work, his thought has inspired fresh engagement with literature and art that he did not explicitly discuss and which, in some senses, was alien to his own critical trajectory. Kaufman, again, has strikingly brought Adorno into dialogue with a range of Romantic writers, particularly William Blake (Kaufman 2000b), Percy Bysshe Shelley (Kaufman 2001a) and John Keats (Kaufman 2001b), and with various modern American poets (Kaufman 2005 and in Gerhardt 2006: 73–118).

J.M. Bernstein's most recent work also stems at least in part from the renewal of the aesthetic and, in particular, from a controversy originally carried on in the pages of the journal *New Left Review* about the political status of aesthetics today (see Beech and Roberts 2002). While Adorno is not mentioned on every other page, his aesthetic theory is developed to impressive effect in Bernstein's *Against Voluptuous Bodies: Late Modernism and the Meaning of Painting*, which seeks to supplement Adorno's own accounts of literary and musical modernism with an account of painterly modernism (Bernstein 2006: 11). In attempting to add to Adorno's authorship in the spirit of Adorno's thought itself, therefore, this is a significant development of aesthetic theory 'after Adorno'. In particular, Bernstein (2006: 7) argues that the arts have become the refuge of significant sensory experience of the world, which otherwise has been damaged in the course taken by modern reason. His work, therefore, represents a serious consideration of the significance assigned to artworks in Adorno's thinking and of the dilapidated state of modern reason that compels real experience to take refuge in art.

CODA

This brief chapter began by commenting on what we might perceive as Adorno's pessimism regarding the future direction of critical thought after him and Horkheimer. If we have emerged at the end of this chapter with the impression that after Adorno there is a thriving tradition of Adorno-interpretation and of currents of thought that continue in his vein, then this is an impression that needs to be qualified. As is often pointed out, Adorno would hardly have relished the increasing celebrity that attaches to his name. This discomfort would not just have been down to modesty. Central to Adorno's thought is its resistance to a situation 'after Adorno' in which his thinking is increasingly taken up, commented upon and celebrated. For a writer who stated that the only reason that we are compelled to philosophize is the continued guilt of existence (ND: 364), the perpetuation of his thinking – even in the most faithful, intelligent and nuanced forms – can hardly be entirely welcome. This is not to say that Adorno would have wished to have been neglected. We must distinguish between what would have been Adorno's wariness with regard to the continued relevance of his work and an imagined – and admittedly bizarre – wish on his part to be ignored. As he intimated near the beginning of *Philosophy of New Music*, there is a subtle but crucial difference between the death of art and its end. The latter will come about when art's promise of happiness is realized; the former, which constantly threatens, occurs when the suggestion that it might be possible for happiness one day to come about is simply suppressed in the interest of preserving things as they are. Adorno's philosophy is conceived against this suppression so that, perhaps, the *promise* of happiness may one day truly be fulfilled in the achievement of happiness itself.

FURTHER READING

WORKS BY THEODOR ADORNO

Adorno wrote the great majority of his works in German. Many of his most important books have now been translated into English, some more successfully than others. The standard edition of Adorno's works in German is the *Gesammelte Schriften*, 20 vols, ed. by Rolf Tiedemann, with Gretel Adorno and Susan Buck-Morss (Frankfurt am Main: Suhrkamp, 1970–86). The ongoing edition of Adorno's posthumous works, some of which have been translated into English and published by Polity Press, is the *Nachgelassene Schriften* (Frankfurt am Main: Suhrkamp, 1993–).

The emphasis that is rightly often placed on the inadequacy of some of the English translations of Adorno's work does not necessarily indicate that his authorship is closed off to English readers or that it is available only in fatally damaged form. This is not least the case because recent years have seen the publication of revised translations of some of the most important books, including *Dialectic of Enlightenment, Philosophy of New Music* and *Aesthetic Theory*. A new translation of *Negative Dialectics*, by Robert Hullot-Kentor, is also scheduled to appear soon. The following is a list of and brief commentary on Adorno's most important works available in English, followed by a similar list of some of the most prominent and useful secondary literature. After the titles of Adorno's works, I have given the date of original publication in square brackets, before giving the date of publication of the relevant edition in the normal way. In the case of posthumous publication, this is clearly indicated;

in the case of collections of essays and articles, the range of dates from the earliest to latest item included in the collection is given in brackets.

This is not a complete list but a guide to help you orientate your initial reading of Adorno and of the secondary literature on his work. You can find a more complete bibliography in *The Cambridge Companion to Adorno*, ed. by Tom Huhn (Cambridge: Cambridge University Press, 2004), 395–420.

Articles

For collections of articles and essays, see under 'Books'.

'The Actuality of Philosophy' [1931] (1977), *Telos*, 31, 120–33. This was Adorno's first lecture as a member of staff to the Faculty of Philosophy at Frankfurt University. It is crucial, therefore, to his early attempt to challenge currently fashionable modes of philosophical thinking, especially Heidegger's. If you wish to understand what Adorno means by 'philosophy', including the relationship of philosophy to real social change, you will need to study this essay carefully.

'The Idea of Natural-History' [1932] (2006), trans. by Robert Hullot-Kentor, in *Things Beyond Resemblance: Collected Essays on Theodor W. Adorno*, New York: Columbia University Press, 252–69. Delivered as a lecture to the Kant Society in Frankfurt in 1932 (that is, not long after 'The Actuality of Philosophy'), this is another major statement of Adorno's early philosophical programme and thus fundamental for an understanding of the foundations and development of his work. It involves an important attempt to think dialectically through the dichotomy of nature and history. Like 'The Actuality of Philosophy', it also evinces a profound debt to, and attempt to grapple with, Benjamin's thinking. Hullot-Kentor's introductory essay in the same volume (234–51) is well worth consulting.

Books

Kierkegaard: Construction of the Aesthetic [1933] (1989; reprint 1999), trans. by Robert Hullot-Kentor, Theory and History of Literature, 61, Minneapolis: University of Minnesota Press. Like Adorno's books on Hegel and Husserl (see *Hegel: Three Studies* and *Against Epistemology*, below), this may seem like a rather dry commentary on a figure from the European philosophical tradition in whom you may or may not be interested. It is, in fact, a very important book in Adorno's authorship. Not only is it his first published work, but, as its subtitle suggests, it is significant to his early thinking about the nature of the aesthetic. Most important of all, of course, is the place this book has in Adorno's lifelong engagement with the attempt to overcome idealism.

Dialectic of Enlightenment: Philosophical Fragments [1947] (2002), ed. by Gunzelin Schmid Noerr, trans. Edmund Jephcott, Stanford, CA: Stanford University Press. This book is still often viewed as the most important work in first-generation Critical Theory. Its diagnosis of the implication of rationalized society with the barbarism from which it imagines itself to have been emancipated certainly set the terms for a great deal of subsequent debate in continental social and cultural studies. The form of the book is, as its subtitle states, fragmentary. It develops its thesis of the entanglement of myth and enlightenment through discussions of a pivotal episode from Homer's *Odyssey*, of the fulfilment of Enlightened morality in the novels of the Marquis de Sade, of the culture industry – indeed, this chapter is central to the development of Adorno's cultural theory – and of anti-Semitism, in a chapter which was significant for the direction of the Frankfurt School during and towards the end of the 1940s. The book ends with a number of notes and fragments that touch on various concerns central to the subsequent work of both Adorno and Horkheimer. In general, the new translation has some significant advantages over the older version by John Cumming (London: Verso, 1979), although the latter is far from worthless, and in some cases its rendering of the German is preferable. On balance, though, use the Jephcott translation.

Philosophy of New Music [1948] (2006), trans. by Robert Hullot-Kentor, Minneapolis: University of Minnesota Press. In importance to Adorno's aesthetics, this book is second only to *Aesthetic Theory*. While the essay on Schoenberg is the earliest text, the 'Introduction' is one of the most insightful statements of Adorno's aesthetic theory, and the essay on Stravinsky is a significant attempt to differentiate the competing trajectories of new music. This book anticipates *Aesthetic Theory* directly in some of its most striking formulations about, for example, the relation of music – and of art generally – to knowledge, about the problem of the social significance of art, about the relation of the musical subject to objective material, and about the relation of form to content.

Minima Moralia [1951] (1974; reprint 2000), trans. by Edmund Jephcott, London: Verso. This is a remarkable book and, although it is hardly 'introductory', it might be a good place to start reading Adorno's published work. His record of despair at the descent into hell during the Second World

War, and of the hope for the revolutionary change of the world that none the less faintly remains, is where I properly began my engagement with Adorno's work. Its chief concern is with the possibility or impossibility of moral philosophy – and, indeed, of the 'good life' at all – today. But here, perhaps more than anywhere else, Adorno's interrelation of moral philosophy, aesthetics, epistemology, psychology and metaphysics, not to mention the most minute attention to individual experience, can keenly be felt.

Prisms [1955] (1981), trans. by Samuel Weber and Shierry Weber, Cambridge, MA: MIT Press. This book, the first of Adorno's German works to be translated into English, brings together both examples of his cultural and literary criticism and his reflections on cultural criticism as such. The opening essay, 'Cultural Criticism and Society', is fundamental to Adorno's work, and the reflections on Benjamin, Kafka and Schoenberg are important documents in Adorno's engagement with some of those figures most important to his intellectual formation.

Against Epistemology: A Metacritique: Studies in Husserl and the Phenomenolgical Antinomies [1956] (1982), trans. by Willis Domingo, Oxford: Basil Blackwell. Growing out of Adorno's doctoral work in Oxford on the phenomenology of Edmund Husserl, this is both an important book on that thinker and a significant work in its own right. Adorno develops a number of ideas which were to become increasingly important to the direction of his thought here, including, in particular, the ideas of immanent critique and of the consequences of this for philosophical method. (I noted earlier that the title of the English translation is somewhat misleading: *Towards a Metacritique of Epistemology* would have been better.)

Hegel: Three Studies [1963] (1993), trans. by Shierry Weber Nicholsen, Cambridge, MA: MIT Press. This book brings together three discussions of Hegel's work: 'Aspects of Hegel's Philosophy', 'The Experiential Content of Hegel's Philosophy' and 'Skoteinos, or How to Read Hegel'. (*Skoteinos* is a Greek word, meaning 'dark' or 'in darkness'.) As well as adding up to an illuminating, distinctive critical interpretation of at least the most important aspects of Hegel's work, this is a major work in the development of Adorno's philosophical thought itself. In dialogue with Hegel, Adorno elaborates his conceptions of philosophical language, of the relation of philosophy to actuality and, perhaps most important of all, of dialectic. This book is both one of the best pieces of twentieth-century Hegel-interpretation and a major philosophical work in its own right.

Negative Dialectics [1966] (1973; reprint 2000), trans. E.B. Ashton, London: Routledge. Although Adorno would have baulked at such a description, this is a magisterial work. Along with *Aesthetic Theory*, it is the most important, thoroughgoing statement of his philosophy. For sure, it is difficult, and some knowledge of Hegel and Heidegger in particular would certainly be helpful in reading it. This is not to say, however, that you shouldn't open this book unless you already have a sound grasp of the Western philosophical tradition. The long 'Introduction' is central to any understanding of Adorno's view of philosophical thought; later sections, through engagements with Heidegger and Kant, are crucial to the account of 'freedom' that Adorno develops; the last chapter is the brilliant 'Meditations on Metaphysics', which is essential reading for anyone interested in Adorno's view of the possibility of thinking in the wake of barbarity.

Aesthetic Theory [posthumously published, 1970] (1997; reprint 1999), trans. by Robert Hullot-Kentor, London: Athlone. This book is central to Adorno's thought, not just regarding art and aesthetics, but generally. In it, he attempts to respond to the situation of Modernist art in which 'It is self-evident that nothing concerning art is self-evident anymore' (AT: 1). Adorno's wish to compose an aesthetic theory that is both philosophical and attentive to art means that he draws on a vast range of artists and philosophers here, from Baudelaire and Beethoven to Kant and Hegel, to give only the most prominent examples. Again, as with *Negative Dialectics*, unfamiliarity with this tradition of artistic production and philosophical reflection does not disqualify the new reader from dealing competently with this book. The 'Draft Introduction' is perhaps a good place to start and Robert Hullot-Kentor's 'Translator's Introduction' gives some useful information about the text and about the previous translation of it.

The Culture Industry: Selected Essays on Mass Culture [1938–69] (1991), ed. by J.M. Bernstein, London: Routledge. Spanning Adorno's career, the essays in this collection (which was not published as a collection by Adorno himself, although the texts included do approach a coherent whole) form the backbone of his controversial theory of culture. Roughly the first half of the book contains some of Adorno's most sustained accounts of the way in which the culture industry is implicated in society ('Culture and Administration'), the dissolution both of work and response in the culture industry ('On the Fetish Character in Music and the Regression of Listening' and 'The Schema of Mass Culture') and the association of the culture industry with fascist propaganda. The second half of the volume includes some important shorter essays from the later part of Adorno's life. In particular, his consideration of 'Free Time' is well worth consulting, as is his carefully argued response to the charge of political disengagement, 'Resignation'. J.M. Bernstein provides a very helpful and insightful 'Introduction', in which he patiently but firmly rebuts postmodern celebrations of mass culture from an Adornian perspective.

The Stars Down to Earth and Other Essays on the Irrational in Culture [1941–53] (1994; reprint 2002), ed. by Stephen Crook, London: Routledge. This collection includes Adorno's essay on the *Los Angeles Times* astrology column as well as some shorter works, including the 'Theses against Occultism', excerpted from *Minima Moralia*, and two discussions of anti-Semitism. This book is a good introduction to a number of features of Adorno's critique of contemporary culture in particular and of irrationality in supposedly rationalized society more generally. Stephen Crook's useful 'Introduction', which draws on a wide range of cultural theory after Adorno, is worth reading, particularly for its considerations of what might seem Adorno's outlandish association of fascist propaganda with the culture industry, and of the continued relevance of Adorno's account of the irrationality of society.

The Positivist Dispute in German Sociology ['Sociology and Empirical Research', first published, 1957; 'Introduction', first published, 1969] (1976), trans. by Glyn Adey and David Frisby, London: Heinemann. Adorno contributed the 'Introduction' and the essay 'Sociology and Empirical Research' to this book. It is worth consulting not just for Adorno's own sociological thought, but for some of the responses to it by more conventional social scientists.

Notes to Literature [1958–65] (1991), 2 vols, trans. by Shierry Weber Nicholsen, New York: Columbia University Press. These two volumes contain most of Adorno's significant literary criticism. They are, therefore, essential reading for anyone interested in his view of literature in particular, and in his aesthetics more generally. Some of Adorno's most important essays – 'The Essay as Form', 'On Lyric Poetry and Society', 'The Artist as Deputy' and 'Commitment' – are included here. While these essays would be central to any reading of Adorno's aesthetics, the shorter texts and fragments should not be neglected. Adorno's reflections on 'Punctuation Marks' and his 'Bibliographical Musings', for only two examples, warrant close consideration. You will also find here Adorno's profound engagements with some of those writers most important to his own development, including the novelist Marcel Proust (1871–1922), the poet and critic Paul Valéry (1871–1945), Samuel Beckett and, of course, Walter Benjamin.

Critical Models: Interventions and Catchwords [*Interventions* (*Eingriffe*), 1963; *Catchwords* (*Stichworte*), 1969] (2005), trans. by Henry W. Pickford, New York: Columbia University Press. This collection of 'critical models', which includes short essays, radio talks and lectures, might be another good place to start your study of Adorno. While many of the texts here might be classified as more introductory than some of Adorno's other published work, they certainly deal with a number of the topics central to his thinking. The essays on the nature of philosophy and on the situation of philosophical thought after the trauma of the Second World War are especially important.

Problems of Moral Philosophy [lectures delivered, 1963; posthumously published, 1996] (2000), trans. by Rodney Livingstone, Cambridge: Polity. Adorno's lectures offer a good point of entry into his work, not least because they often deal in much simpler terms than his published books with some of the most pressing concerns of his thought. (This is not to say, of course, that a reading of the lectures can substitute for a reading of the published work.) Perhaps the most significant set of lectures so far published in English is the *Problems of Moral Philosophy* because they give us some sense of the book on moral philosophy that Adorno had planned to write but which he did not live to complete. These lectures offer an original and nuanced reading of Kant's main works in moral philosophy and represent an extensive gloss on Adorno's statement that 'there is no right life in wrong life'. The other sets of lectures so far available in English are *Kant's Critique of Pure Reason*, *History and Freedom*, *Metaphysics: Concept and Problems* and *Introduction to Sociology*, all published by Polity.

WORKS ON THEODOR ADORNO

Articles and chapters in books

Articles on Adorno appear frequently in journals such as *Critical Inquiry*, *New German Critique*, *Constellations*, *European Journal of Philosophy* and, indeed, almost anywhere else. This is a handful of significant examples of some of the recent work on Adorno. Again, a fuller list can be found in *The Cambridge Companion to Adorno*.

Ferris, David S. (2005), 'Politics and the Enigma of Art: The Meaning of Modernism for Adorno', *Modernist Cultures*, 1, 192–208 (available at: <http://www.js-modcult.bham.ac.uk/editor/welcome.asp>). This is an extremely nuanced account of Adorno's view of Modernist art as the intensification of artistic autonomy. It also deals, very subtly, with Adorno's reception of Kant's aesthetics.

Habermas, Jürgen [1985] (1987), 'The Entwinement of Myth and Enlightenment: Max Horkheimer and Theodor Adorno', in *The Philosophical Discourse of Modernity: Twelve Lectures*, trans. by Frederick Lawrence, Cambridge: Polity: A careful reading of *Dialectic of Enlightenment* in which some of the characteristic objections levelled by subsequent generations of the Frankfurt School against Adorno's alleged pessimism are set out. Important reading for anyone wishing to grasp the reception of Adorno's thought.

Jarvis, Simon (2004), 'What is Speculative Thinking?', *Revue internationale de philosophie*, 63, 69–83. On the one hand, this is an attempt to reconsider Adorno's relationship to an important aspect of Hegel's philosophy. On the other, it is a detailed account of what 'thinking' is, according to Adorno. In particular, Jarvis emphasizes the way that, for Adorno, thinking must involve bodily experience in order to be thinking at all. In this way, this article develops an important strand of Jarvis's earlier book on Adorno (see below).

Kaufman, Robert (2000a), 'Red Kant, or The Persistence of the Third Critique in Adorno and Jameson', *Critical Inquiry*, 26, 682–724. This is a long and exacting account not just of Adorno's interpretation of Kant's aesthetics – and of Jameson's reading of that interpretation – but of 'the aesthetic' in Adorno as such. It is central to Kaufman's attempt to re-envisage Adorno's aesthetic theory as the '[reworking] of Kant – into a late modernist, Left vocabulary'.

—— (2005), 'Lyric's Constellation, Poetry's Radical Privilege', *Modernist Cultures*, 1, 209–33 (available at <http://www.js-modcult.bham.ac.uk/editor/welcome.asp>) Along with Kaufman's essay in *The Cambridge Companion to Adorno*, this is an important consideration of the significance of Adorno's considerations of lyric poetry. This essay develops an Adornian reading of the American poet Robert Duncan (1919–88). Compare it to Kaufman's essays on Adorno and Shelley, and on Adorno and modern poetry, available at Romantic Circles Praxis Series (<http://www.rc.umd.edu/praxis/>).

Pepper, Thomas Adam (1997), 'Guilt by (Un)free Association: Adorno on Romance *et al.*, with Some Reference to the Schlock Experience', in *Singularities: Extremes of Theory in the Twentieth Century*, Cambridge: Cambridge

University Press. Sometimes irritatingly pretentious, this is also a virtuosic and, in some regards, well-informed reading of *Minima Moralia*, especially of its conception of love, which Pepper contends is owed in some part to Adorno's reading of Kierkegaard.

Rothberg, Michael (2000), 'After Adorno: Culture in the Wake of Catastrophe', in *Traumatic Realism: The Demands of Holocaust Representation*, Minneapolis: University of Minnesota Press. This is a precise but sympathetic account of the various misreadings to which Adorno's dictum that 'to write poetry after Auschwitz is barbaric' has been subjected. As well as discussing the range and importance of Adorno's influence on thinking about the consequences of the Holocaust, Rothberg offers an innovative reading of Adorno's comments themselves.

Books

Bernstein, J.M. (2001), *Adorno: Disenchantment and Ethics*, Cambridge: Cambridge University Press. Bernstein's work on Adorno is some of the best there is. This book is both ambitious and intricate, and shows remarkable clarity of thought and expression. Bernstein first gives a detailed reading of Adorno's most prominent works in moral philosophy, especially *Minima Moralia*, before moving on to a reconstruction of what an Adornian moral theory might look like. It is remarkable that in such a textually detailed book Adorno's work is frequently brought into dialogue with a range of other moral philosophies, especially those of Kant and Hegel, but also virtue ethics and utilitarianism. This book is highly recommended both for those interested in the potential of Adorno's work for moral philosophy, and for those concerned to get a more nuanced grip on his philosophy more generally. Readers especially interested in the development of Adorno's ethical theory and in responses to Habermas's criticisms of him should also consult Bernstein's earlier *Recovering Ethical Life: Jürgen Habermas and the Future of Critical Theory* (1995).

—— (2006), *Against Voluptuous Bodies: Late Modernism and the Meaning of Painting*, Stanford, CA: Stanford University Press. This develops aspects of Adorno's aesthetics – and of his and Horkheimer's account of modern rationality more broadly – in the direction of a provocative reading of late Modernist painting. While, by Bernstein's own admission, Adorno's name is far from being mentioned on every other page, this book's thesis that Modernist painting aims at the redemption of the material world, which has been deadened by modern rationality, represents a major engagement with and application of Adorno's thinking.

Dews, Peter (1987; reprint 2007), *Logics of Disintegration: Post-Structuralist Thought and the Claims of Critical Theory*, London: Verso. The title of this book is borrowed from *Negative Dialectics*. In it, Dews outlines some of the ways in which the French philosopher Jacques Derrida (1930–2004), who was perhaps the main figure associated with post-structuralism and deconstruction, struggled to make post-structuralism 'practico-political' (Derrida quoted on p. 42). Dews argues that, for Derrida, truth is always a matter for metaphysics and that as part of this assumption there is in Derrida's thought 'the equation of truth and coercive identity' (p. 53). Adorno's conception of the relationship between philosophy and political practice, Dews argues, enables a move beyond this position.

Gerhardt, Christina, ed. (2006), 'Adorno and Ethics', special issue of *New German Critique*, 97. Bringing together papers presented at a conference on 'Adorno and Ethics' in 2003, this volume is a major contribution to the scholarship on Adorno's moral philosophy, which has recently emerged as a significant topic in the discussion of his work. All of the essays are worth consulting; under-elaborated topics in Adorno's thinking are explored by Gandesha (Adorno's theory of language) and Gerhardt (the role of animals in Adorno's thinking). García Düttmann's sensitive account of the controversies in which Adorno was involved is worth reading.

Gibson, Nigel and Andrew Rubin, eds (2002), *Adorno: A Critical Reader*, Oxford: Blackwell. This useful collection of critical essays focuses largely on Adorno's cultural theory and aesthetics, especially his musicology, although some important discussion of his philosophy and social theory, including an essay on sexuality in his thinking, is also included. Edward Said's influential article on 'Adorno as Lateness Itself' is reprinted here. There is an extremely extensive bibliography, especially of Adorno's own works.

Habermas, Jürgen [1981] (1984 and 1987), *The Theory of Communicative Action*, vol. I: *Reason and the Rationalization of Society*, and vol. II: *Lifeworld and System: A Critique of Functionalist Reason*, trans. by Thomas McCarthy, Boston, MA: Beacon Press. Perhaps the most important work of second-generation Critical Theory, this is not so much a book on Adorno but one that is nevertheless indispensable to any understanding of how his work has been taken up and criticized by subsequent generations of thinkers. Many readers will want to question Habermas's reconstruction of Adorno's (and

Horkheimer's) thought, as well as his own optimism about the prospects for theoretical knowledge.

Hammer, Espen (2006), *Adorno and the Political*, London: Routledge. Hammer's book is both a very thorough and fresh account of those aspects of Adorno's political thinking central to his work and, especially in the final chapter, an attempt to consider some of the ways in which Adorno's thought might relate to political concerns not usually viewed as important to him, such as, in particular, feminism and ecology. This book is a very good introduction, therefore, to all aspects of Adorno's political thinking, as well as a novel elaboration of many of them.

Hohendahl, Peter Uwe (1995), *Prismatic Thought: Theodor W. Adorno*, Lincoln: University of Nebraska Press. This is another overall introduction to Adorno's thought, with some commentary on 'Critical Theory after Adorno' at the end. There is a particular focus on art, especially literature, and an important discussion of Adorno's views on the nature of language.

Honneth, Axel [1985] (1991), *The Critique of Power: Reflective Stages in Critical Social Theory*, trans. by Kenneth Baynes, Cambridge, MA: MIT Press. Honneth takes earlier Critical Theory to task because of what he perceives as the inability in it to articulate an adequate theory of society. He focuses in particular on the way in which the individual is conceived by Adorno and Horkheimer, charging that they do not pay sufficient attention to the relationship between individual and society. Adorno's position is 'resignative' in the sense that it gives up the possibility of empirical social theory. Honneth develops aspects of Habermas's thought in order to propose solutions to some of the problems he sees in Adorno.

Huhn, Tom, ed. (2004), *The Cambridge Companion to Adorno*, Cambridge: Cambridge University Press. This thick compendium of essays on most aspects of Adorno's authorship is an essential resource for anyone seriously interested in his work. Some of the essays set Adorno in his intellectual and historical context (for example, Gandesha and Schmidt on Adorno in exile); there are a number of essays which develop fresh perspectives on important questions arising from Adorno's philosophy (including Jarvis on materialism and Bernstein on dialectic); and others draw our attention to heretofore underexamined aspects of Adorno's work (especially Tiedemann on Adorno's never-completed opera). Other essays discuss different areas of Adorno's work, such as Robert Kaufman's study of Adorno's literary criticism. The essays by Menke and Schweppenhäuser are extremely significant documents in the renewed interest in Adorno's moral theory. The bibliography is very thorough.

Huhn, Tom and Lambert Zuidervaart, eds (1997), *The Semblance of Subjectivity: Essays in Adorno's Aesthetic Theory*, Cambridge, MA: MIT Press. This is a very helpful collection of essays on most aspects of Adorno's aesthetic theory. There are some useful pieces on Adorno's relation to other twentieth-century thinkers (Jay on a point of possible comparison with Philippe Lacoue-Labarthe (1940–2007); Nicholsen and Wolin on the debt to Benjamin), whereas Huhn's account of Adorno's reception of Kant's aesthetics is extremely significant if, ultimately, contestable. There are some excellent considerations both of prominent but intractable concerns in Adorno's thinking (Bernstein's essay on 'semblance' is a major contribution to the literature on Adorno's aesthetic theory) and of less frequently considered aspects and consequences of his authorship. The translation of Rüdiger Bubner's important and controversial essay on the relationship between aesthetics and theory in Adorno is also valuable. This book has a very thorough bibliography, especially for Adorno's aesthetic and cultural theory.

Hullot-Kentor, Robert (2006), *Things beyond Resemblance: Collected Essays on Theodor W. Adorno*, New York: Columbia University Press. Hullot-Kentor, translator of *Philosophie der neuen Musik*, *Ästhetische Theorie*, *Kierkegaard* and a number of important essays by Adorno, has written widely on various aspects of Adorno's thought. This is a collection of some of his most important essays, including some consideration of the precise relevance of Adorno's thought to contemporary American society. Hullot-Kentor's translation of 'The Idea of Natural-History' is also included here.

Jameson, Fredric (1990), *Late Marxism: Adorno, or, The Persistence of the Dialectic*, London: Verso. Jameson is a prominent literary theorist and critic in his own right and this is an enormously influential book for the reception of Adorno in Anglophone literary theory and criticism. There has been some attempt recently to distance Anglophone Adorno scholarship from Jameson (by Hullot-Kentor most vociferously, and by Kaufman), but Jameson's book remains important to the English-speaking reception of Adorno's thought.

Jarvis, Simon (1998), *Adorno: A Critical Introduction*, Cambridge: Polity. This is one of the best books on Adorno in recent years. On the one hand, it offers a very detailed introduction to most aspects of Adorno's thought. It is probably the next item of critical literature on Adorno that should be read after finishing this book, therefore. On the other hand, it develops an original interpretation of Adorno's philosophical significance by carefully placing his thought in the context of classical German philosophy. It includes nuanced accounts of Adorno's relation to Kant and Hegel, in particular. One of the main aims of Jarvis's work on Adorno is to show that precisely when those aspects of Adorno's thinking that have been judged to be obsolete – especially by subsequent generations of Critical Theorists – are discarded, then much of the force of Adorno's philosophy is also lost.

Jay, Martin (1984), *Adorno*, London: Fontana. Perhaps superseded now by later introductory works, this short book is still an important work in the history of the reception of Adorno's thought. It gives a useful overview of the central aspects of Adorno's authorship.

Müller-Doohm, Stefan (2005), *Adorno: A Biography*, trans. by Rodney Livingstone, Cambridge: Polity. Müller-Doohm is fully apprised of the wariness with which Adorno would have met any biography of himself, and not just because of the natural anxiety to shield parts of his life from public scrutiny. Müller-Doohm's book is a compendious guide to Adorno's intellectual development, his intellectual and personal relationships, his professional career, and institutional affiliations. A great deal of material relating to everything from Adorno's early music criticism in the vibrant Frankfurt of the 1920s to his traumatic confrontation with the student movement of the late 1960s is marshalled. In particular, Müller-Doohm does a good job of elaborating the development of Adorno's social theory (Müller-Doohm has also written a book, as yet untranslated, on Adorno's sociology). Of course, there are the quirky details – such as Adorno's offer to purchase a pair of wombats for Frankfurt Zoo – but the main contribution of this massive book is in its exhaustiveness and its occasionally revealing contextualization of important aspects of Adorno's thought.

Rose, Gillian (1978), *The Melancholy Science: An Introduction to the Thought of Theodor W. Adorno*, London: Macmillan. This is a very important work in the Anglophone reception of Adorno's thought. It is a remarkably thoroughgoing account of most aspects of Adorno's thought, especially, in the central chapters, of Adorno's explicitly social and philosophical works. The remarks on the stylistic aspect of *Minima Moralia* are perhaps particularly valuable. Hard to track down these days, but well worth the effort.

Wellmer, Albrecht [1985 and 1986] (1991), *The Persistence of Modernity: Essays on Aesthetics, Ethics and Postmodernism*, trans. by David Midgley, Cambridge: Polity. This collection brings together translations of some of Wellmer's most important essays on Adorno, especially his 'Truth, Semblance, Reconciliation', on Adorno's aesthetics, and 'The Dialectic of Modernism and Postmodernism', which aims to develop aspects of Habermas's criticism of Adorno's allegedly undue pessimism. Wellmer is particularly keen to push Habermas's suggestion that Critical Theory must change its paradigm from the philosophy of consciousness to the philosophy of language.

Zuidervaart, Lambert (1991), *Adorno's Aesthetic Theory: The Redemption of Illusion*, Cambridge, MA: MIT Press. This book would serve as a good companion to a thorough study of *Aesthetic Theory*. Zuidervaart's book is an extremely thorough account of *Aesthetic Theory*, of Adorno's aesthetic, literary and musical philosophy more broadly, and of a number of central concerns of his philosophy in general. Its rigorous commentary is complemented by equally rigorous consideration of objections to various aspects of Adorno's thought. Zuidervaart does a good job of arguing for the cogency of some of the most controversial and prominent features of Adorno's aesthetic theory, including, in particular, his notion of the truth of works of art.

Internet resources

I list here only those internet resources that seem, to me, to be the most helpful. Adorno now has a considerable presence on the internet, but much of this material needs to be approached with caution. The following websites, however, offer important information, and, in some cases, illuminating interpretation of Adorno's work.

<http://plato.stanford.edu/entries/adorno/>. This is the entry on Adorno in the (sometimes) helpful *Stanford Dictionary of Philosophy*. It is written by Lambert Zuidervaart, a respected Adorno scholar, and contains extensive discussions of most aspects of Adorno's work as well as a thorough bibliography.

<http://www.grovemusic.com/shared/views/article.html?section=music .00216>. *The Grove Music Encyclopaedia* is the authoritative reference work for the study of music. Its article on Adorno, by Max Paddison, who has written widely on Adorno's musicology, is very useful, giving detailed information about Adorno's musical development and interests. The bibliography is also well worth consulting, especially for those interested in Adorno's aesthetics and musicology.

<http://www.ifs.uni-frankfurt.de/index.html>. This is the website of the Institute for Social Research at Frankfurt University. It gives exhaustive information (in German) about the institute's current programme and research projects, as well as its history. Detailed summaries in English of the institute's programme (under *Programm*) and history (under *Geschichte*) are available. There is also a thorough list of the institute's publications. This would be a good place to start initial research into the very latest developments of Critical Theory in the wake of Adorno.

WORKS CITED

Only those works not already listed in 'Further Reading' are included here. As in 'Further Reading', I have included the date of original publication in square brackets before the date of publication of the edition used wherever there is a significant difference between these dates.

Agamben, Giorgio (1998), *Homo Sacer: Sovereign Power and Bare Life*, trans. by Daniel Heller-Roazen, Stanford, CA: Stanford University Press

—— (1999), *The Man without Content*, trans. by Georgia Albert, Stanford, CA: Stanford University Press

Beckett, Samuel [1958] (1990), *Endgame*, in *The Complete Dramatic Works*, London: Faber and Faber, 89–134

Beech, David and John Roberts, eds (2002), *The Philistine Controversy*, London: Verso

Benjamin, Walter [1920] (1996a; reprint 2000), 'The Concept of Criticism in German Romanticism', trans. by David Lachterman, Howard Eiland and Ian Balfour, in *Walter Benjamin: Selected Writings*, Vol. I: *1913–1926*, Cambridge, MA: Belknap Press, 116–200

—— [1921] (1996b; reprint 2000), 'Critique of Violence', trans. by Edmund Jephcott, in *Walter Benjamin: Selected Writings*, Vol. I, *1913–1926*, Cambridge, MA: Belknap Press, 236–52

—— [1928] (1998; reprint 2003), *The Origin of German Tragic Drama*, trans. by John Osborne, London: Verso

Bloch, Ernst [first edition, 1918; second edition, 1923] (2000), *The Spirit of Utopia*, trans. by Anthony A. Nassar, Stanford, CA: Stanford University Press

Caygill, Howard (1998), *Walter Benjamin: The Colour of Experience*, London: Routledge

Dubiel, Helmut (1992), 'Domination or Emancipation? The Debate over the Heritage of Critical Theory', in *Cultural–Political Interventions in the Unfinished Project of Enlightenment*, ed. by Axel Honneth *et al.*, Cambridge, MA: MIT Press

Eagleton, Terry (1990), *The Ideology of the Aesthetic*, Oxford: Basil Blackwell

Freud, Sigmund [1900] (1976), *The Interpretation of Dreams*, ed. by Angela Richards, trans. by James Strachey, Penguin Freud Library, 4, London: Penguin

Genette, Gérard (1999), *The Aesthetic Relation*, trans. by G.M. Goshgarian, Ithaca: Cornell University Press

Geuss, Raymond (1981), *The Idea of a Critical Theory: Habermas and the Frankfurt School*, Cambridge: Cambridge University Press

—— (2005), *Outside Ethics*, Princeton, NJ: Princeton University Press

Glaister, Dan (2006), 'Hollywood Gets a New Role as Los Angeles' Great Polluter', *Guardian*, 15 November, 19

Hegel, G.W.F. [1807] (1977), *Phenomenology of Spirit*, trans. by A.V. Miller, Oxford: Oxford University Press

—— [1821] (1991; reprint 1998) *Elements of the Philosophy of Right*, ed. by Allen W. Wood, trans. by H.B. Nisbet, Cambridge: Cambridge University Press

—— [lectures delivered, 1820–9; posthumously published, 1835] (1975a; reprint 1988) *Aesthetics: Lectures on Fine Art*, trans. by T.M. Knox, 2 vols, Oxford: Clarendon Press

—— [1830] (1975b) *Hegel's Logic*, trans. by William Wallace, 3rd edn, Oxford: Clarendon Press

Heidegger, Martin [1927] (1962; reprint 2000) *Being and Time*, trans. by John Macquarrie and Edward Robinson, Oxford: Blackwell

Horkheimer, Max [1942] (1987), 'Vernunft und Selbsterhaltung', *Gesammelte Schriften*, ed. by Alfred Schmidt and Gunzelin Schmid Noerr, Frankfurt-am-Main: Fischer, V, 320–50

—— [1931] (1993), 'The Present Situation of Social Philosophy and the Tasks of an Institute for Social Research', in *Between Philosophy and Social Science: Selected Early Writings*, trans. by G. Frederick Hunter, Matthew S. Kramer and John Torpey, Cambridge, MA: MIT Press, 1–14

Huxley, Aldous [1921] (2004), *Crome Yellow*, London: Vintage

Ibsen, Henrik [1884] (1960), *The Wild Duck*, in *Ibsen, VI: An Enemy of the People, The Wild Duck, Rosmersholm*, trans. by James Walter McFarlane, London: Oxford University Press

Inwood, Michael (1992; reprint 1998), *A Hegel Dictionary*, Oxford: Blackwell

Joyce, James (1939), *Finnegans Wake*, London: Faber

Kant, Immanuel [first edition, 1781; second edition, 1787] (1997), *Critique of Pure Reason*, ed. and trans. by Paul Guyer and Allen W. Wood, Cambridge: Cambridge University Press

—— [1784] (1996a; reprint 1999) 'What is Enlightenment?', in *Practical Philosophy*, ed. and trans. by Mary J. Gregor, Cambridge: Cambridge University Press, 15–22

—— [1785] (1996b; 1999), *Groundwork of the Metaphysics of Morals*, in *Practical Philosophy*, ed. and trans. by Mary J. Gregor, Cambridge: Cambridge University Press, 41–108

—— [1790] (2000; reprint 2001), *Critique of the Power of Judgement*, ed. by Paul Guyer, trans. by Paul Guyer and Eric Matthews, Cambridge: Cambridge University Press

Kaufman, Robert (2000b), 'Everybody Hates Kant: Blakean Formalism and the Symmetries of Laura Moriarty', *Modern Language Quarterly*, 61, 132–55

Kaufman, Robert (2001a), 'Intervention and Commitment Forever! Shelley in 1819, Shelley in Brecht, Shelley in Adorno, Shelley in Benjamin', *Romantic Circles Praxis Series*, <http://www.rc.umd.edu/praxis/>

—— (2001b), 'Negatively Capable Dialectics: Keats, Vendler, Adorno, and the Theory of the Avant-Garde', *Critical Inquiry*, 27, 354–84

Kennedy, Paul (1989), *The Rise and Fall of the Great Powers: Economic Change and Military Conflict from 1500 to 2000*, London: Fontana

Lukács, Georg [1916] (1971a; reprint 2003), *The Theory of the Novel*, trans. by Anna Bostock, London: Merlin

—— [1923] (1971b), *History and Class Consciousness*, trans. by Rodney Livingstone, London: Merlin

Marx, Karl [1844] (1975; reprint 1977), 'Economic and Philosophical Manuscripts', in *Early Writings*, trans. by Rodney Livingstone and Gregor Benton, Harmondsworth: Penguin, 279–400

—— [1867] (1976; reprint 1990), *Capital: A Critique of Political Economy*, vol. I, trans. by Ben Fowkes, London: Harmondsworth

Nietzsche, Friedrich [1876] (1983; reprint 1991), *Untimely Meditations*, trans. by R.J. Hollingdale, Cambridge: Cambridge University Press

—— [1886] (1973; reprint 1990), *Beyond Good and Evil: Prelude to a Philosophy of the Future*, trans. by R.J. Hollingdale, Harmondsworth: Penguin

Reich, Klaus [1932] (1992), *The Completeness of Kant's Table of Judgments*, trans. by Jane Kneller and Michael Losonsky, Stanford, CA: Stanford University Press

Santner, Eric L. (1990), *Stranded Objects: Mourning, Memory, and Film in Postwar Germany*, Ithaca, NY: Cornell University Press

—— (2006), *On Creaturely Life: Rilke, Benjamin, Sebald*, Chicago: University of Chicago Press

Sartre, Jean-Paul [1948] (2001; reprint 2002), *What Is Literature?*, trans. by Bernard Frechtman, London: Routledge

Schlegel, Friedrich [1797] (1967), 'Kritische Fragmente', in *Kritische Friedrich-Schlegel-Ausgabe*, ed. by Ernst Behler, with Jean-Jacques Anstett and Hans Eichner, Munich: Schöningh, II, 147–63

Schnädelbach, Herbert (1984), *Philosophy in Germany, 1831–1933*, trans. by Eric Matthews, Cambridge: Cambridge University Press

Smith, William and John Lockwood (1933; reprint 2004), *Chambers Murray Latin–English Dictionary*, Edinburgh: Chambers; London: Murray

Steiner, George (1967), *Language and Silence: Essays, 1958–1966*, London: Faber

Weber, Max [1904–5] (1930; reprint 2000), *The Protestant Ethic and the Spirit of Capitalism*, trans. by Talcott Parsons, London: Routledge

INDEX

Second Viennese School: *see* music, new
Second World War 57, 78, 79, 84
self-preservation 18–20, 22, 25
September 11th 2001: American and British response to attacks of 77
Shelley, Percy Bysshe 113
Smith, Adam 86
soap 21
society: theory of 2, 62, 77–91
Soviet Union 99–100
Spengler, Oswald 63, 90
Stalin, Joseph: *see* Soviet Union
Steiner, George 111
Stravinsky, Igor 49
Student movement 1, 103
subject and object 17–18, 20–1, 46, 72–3
subjectivity: *see* reason; renunciation; and, subject and object
sublation 68

taste 4, 37–8, 46; autonomy of 37
theology 87, 98–9, 109
theory, and practice 102–4
thought: and freedom 102–4; and impulse 67–9, 75; and pleasure

36–7, 43; universal communicability of 71
truth: *see* knowledge; philosophy; and, truth-content
truth-content 44, 53
Turner, J.M.W.: *Steamer in a Snowstorm* 46

universal: *see* particular
utopia 61, 93, 96–7; negative 96

Vienna Circle 70
vitalism 90
vivisection 16
voodoo 16

Weber, Max: *The Protestant Ethic and the Spirit of Capitalism* 21–2, 39–40
Webern, Anton 49
Wellmer, Albrecht 106, 108–9
work: and pleasure 5, 38–9, 44; *see also* labour; life; and, thought

X-Factor, The 30

Zuidervaart, Lambert 53

Related titles from Routledge

Stuart Hall
James Procter

Stuart Hall is one of the founding figures of cultural studies. He was director of the Centre for Contemporary Cultural Studies, famously coined the term 'Thatcherism', and assessed new Labour as the 'great moving nowhere show'. One of the leading public intellectuals of the postwar period, he has helped transform our understanding of culture as both a theoretical category and a political practice. James Procter's introduction places Hall's work within its historical contexts, providing a clear guide to his key ideas and influences, as well as to his critics and his intellectual legacy, covering topics such as:

- popular culture and youth subcultures
- the CCCS and cultural studies
- media and communication
- racism and resistance
- Thatcherism
- identity, ethnicity, diaspora

Stuart Hall is the ideal gateway to the work of a critic described by Terry Eagleton as 'a walking chronicle of everything from the New Left to New Times, Leavis to Lyotard, Aldermaston to ethnicity'.

ISBN10: 0-415-26266-6 (hbk)
ISBN10: 0-415-26267-4 (pbk)
ISBN10: 0-203-49698-1 (ebk)

ISBN13: 978-0-415-26266-8 (hbk)
ISBN13: 978-0-415-26267-5 (pbk)
ISBN13: 978-0-203-49698-5 (ebk)

Available at all good bookshops
For ordering and further information please visit:
www.routledge.com

Related titles from Routledge

Antonio Gramsci
Steve Jones

Is power simply a matter of domination and resistance? Or can a ruling power be vulnerable; can subordinates find their resistance neutralized; and what is the role of culture in this? Gramsci's work invites people to think beyond simplistic oppositions by recasting ideological domination as hegemony: the ability of a ruling power's values to live in the minds and lives of its subalterns as a spontaneous expression of their own interests. Targeting readers encountering Gramsci for the first time, Steve Jones covers key elements of his thought through detailed discussion of:

*   culture
*   hegemony
*   intellectuals
*   crisis
*   Americanization.

In doing so, *Antonio Gramsci* studies the historical context of the theorist's thought, offers examples of putting Gramsci's ideas into practice in the analysis of contemporary culture and evaluates responses to his work.

ISBN10: 0-415-31947-1 (hbk)
ISBN10: 0-415-31948-X (pbk)
ISBN10: 0-203-62552-8 (ebk)

ISBN13: 978-0-415-31947-8 (hbk)
ISBN13: 978-0-415-31948-5 (pbk)
ISBN13: 978-0-203-62552-1 (ebk)

Available at all good bookshops
For ordering and further information please visit:
www.routledge.com

Related titles from Routledge

Feminist Film Theorists
Shohini Chaudhuri

Since it began in the 1970s, feminist film theory has revolutionized the
way that films and their spectators can be understood. This book focuses
on the groundbreaking work of Laura Mulvey, Kaja Silverman, Teresa de
Lauretis, and Barbara Creed. Each of these thinkers has opened up a new
and distinctive approach to the study of film and this book provides the
most detailed account so far of their ideas. It illuminates the following six
key concepts and demonstrates their value as tools for film analysis:

- the male gaze
- the female voice
- technologies of gender
- queering desire
- the monstrous-feminine
- masculinity in crisis

Shohini Chaudhuri shows how these four thinkers construct their theories
through their reading of films as well as testing their ideas with a number
of other examples from contemporary cinema and television. She
concludes that the concepts have not remained static over the past thirty
years but have continually evolved with the influence of new critical
debates and developments in film production, signalling their continuing
impact and relevance in an era that is often unthinkingly branded as 'post-
feminist'.

ISBN10: 0-415-32432-7 (hbk)
ISBN10: 0-415-32433-5 (pbk)
ISBN10: 0-203-35702-7 (ebk)

ISBN13: 978-0-415-32432-8 (hbk)
ISBN13: 978-0-415-32433-5 (pbk)
ISBN13: 978-0-203-35702-6 (ebk)

Available at all good bookshops
For ordering and further information please visit:
www.routledge.com

Related titles from Routledge

Slavoj Žižek
Tony Myers

Slavoj Žižek is no ordinary thinker. Combining psychoanalysis, philosophy and politics into a compelling whole, Žižek's approach is always both fresh and fascinating. The scope of his subject matter is equally exhilarating, ranging from political apathy of contemporary life, to a joke about the man who thins he will be eaten by a chicken, from the ethical heroism of Keanu Reeves in 'Speed', to what toilet designs reveal about the national psyche. In this volume, Tony Myers provides a clear and engaging guide to Žižek's key ideas, explaining the main influences on Žižek's thought, most crucially his engagement with Lacanian psychoanalysis, using examples drawn from popular culture and everyday life, Myers outlines for the first time the main issues that Žižek's work tackles, including:

- What is a subject and why is it so important?
- What is so terrible about postmodernity?
- How can we distinguish reality from ideology?
- What is the relationship between men and women?
- Why is racism always a fantasy?

Slavoj Žižek is essential reading for anyone wanting to understand the thought of the critic whom Terry Eagleton has described as 'the most formidably brilliant exponent of psychoanalysis, indeed of cultural theory in general, to have emerged in Europe for some decades'.

ISBN10: 0-415-26264-X (hbk)
ISBN10: 0-415-26265-8 (pbk)
ISBN10: 0-203-63440-3 (ebk)

ISBN13: 978-0-415-26264-4 (hbk)
ISBN13: 978-0-415-26265-1 (pbk)
ISBN13: 978-0-203-63440-0 (ebk)

Available at all good bookshops
For ordering and further information please visit:
www.routledge.com